FAMILY GUIDE EMERGENCY HEALTH CARE

A REFERENCE GUIDE FOR STUDENTS OF THE
MEDICAL SELF-HELP TRAINING COURSE

ACKNOWLEDGMENT

We wish to acknowledge with grateful appreciation the many services provided by the American Medical Association, through the Committee on Disaster Medical Care, Council on National Security, Board of Trustees and staff, in the preparation of this handbook.

From the inception of studies to determine emergency health techniques and procedures, the Association gave valuable assistance and support. The Committee on Disaster Medical Care of the Council on National Security, AMA, reviewed the material in its various stages of production, and made significant contributions to the content of the handbook.

INTRODUCTION

Individuals and families have an essential role in national defense—a role that is both simple and complex. Simple because it requires rather elementary preparedness measures on the part of every person. Complex because it demands that each person be ready to *live on his own* for 2 weeks—the period following a nuclear attack when outside assistance might not be available.

The importance of this role becomes readily apparent when one appreciates the fact that the ability of the United States to recover from a nuclear attack and continue as a free and democratic Nation would depend upon its most precious resource: human life. Buildings, machines, powerlines—these could be replaced. But not the individual American.

Obviously, we would be only deceiving ourselves if we were to expound the idea that *all* persons could survive a nuclear attack. Many would be killed by the blast and thermal effects of the weapons. But many others—most Americans—would survive if they had made certain preparations after accepting their personal responsibilities in national defense.

A nuclear attack could deny you access to doctors, nurses, and other medical personnel; hospitals, clinics, drug and grocery stores; normal water, sewerage, fuel, and power services. All of these services and facilities are normally important to the health of your family, and you might have to get along for a time without any of them.

Your problem and responsibility would be: How to maintain health without help.

The purpose of this handbook is to assist you in meeting that responsibility. *The handbook is not intended as a substitute for professional medical care.* It is intended only to help in maintaining health and alleviating suffering during any period of disaster when professional care and normal services might not be available. This handbook is only available to those who have completed the Medical Self Help Training Course.

Some of the preparations you can make for the health of your family in an emergency are as simple as they are important. For example, there are certain supplies you should have on hand. You should make sure that all vaccinations, such as smallpox, tetanus shots, and others recommended by your physician, are kept up to date for all members of the family. These and other preparations should be made now because there would not be time to do them in an emergency.

The handbook covers a wide range of health topics. There is information on treating a toothache; there is also information on childbirth. The space devoted to any one topic is necessarily limited. But every bit of information is aimed at one central theme: Helping you alleviate suffering and sustain life in that critical personal period following a nuclear attack—the first 14 days.

CONTENTS

SECTION I

Part 1 RADIOACTIVE FALLOUT AND SHELTER
Part 2 HEALTHFUL LIVING IN EMERGENCIES

RADIOACTIVE FALLOUT AND SHELTER

A nuclear attack against the United States could start a multitude of health problems. The newest and perhaps strangest of these would be associated with radioactive fallout.

Actually, the only new part of the term "radioactive fallout" is the second word—fallout. Radioactivity is older than man—as old as the cosmic rays and mineral deposits that have given off nuclear radiation for centuries, long unnoticed by man and of no general concern to him. The problem, then, is *fallout*, a modern term to describe a modern threat. The single explanation of this complex danger is in the term itself: It is a danger that could *fall out* upon man and his environment—the newest airborne weapon of the nuclear age.

Nuclear weapons were developed for just one purpose—to make military use of the tremendous energy and explosive power in the atom. This power was demonstrated at Hiroshima and Nagasaki, and it ended World War II. But about 9 years later a series of nuclear tests in the Pacific focused attention on another atomic danger: radioactive fallout. The test results supported the theories of a few, surprised many, and brought a new threat to millions, for they planted the seeds that grew into this fact: In a nuclear attack, this thing called fallout could endanger more people than the blast and heat from the nuclear explosions.

Solutions to the problems associated with the fallout threat start with the answer to three questions: What is fallout? What are some of the protective measures against fallout radiation? What are the effects of radiation on humans?

RADIOACTIVE FALLOUT

The detonation of a nuclear weapon near the surface of the ground results in four major effects: (1) blast (2) heat (3) initial radiation, and (4) residual radiation. The first three effects can cause severe damage over a broad but limited area—broad when compared with the area of damage from conventional weapons in World War II, and limited when compared with the area that could be endangered by radioactive fallout. For example, a ten-megaton * nuclear burst at ground level could result in effects generally as follows:

1. Blast—Would destroy most buildings 5 miles from the point of explosion. The destruction 7 miles away would be less severe,

---

*A 10-megaton weapon has the explosive power of 10 million tons of TNT.

but injuries would be high, caused by flying debris (about 150 square miles of damage).

2. Heat—Severe damage and heat capable of causing second-degree burns (on the bare skin of persons in the open) over an area with a radius of about 18 miles from the point of explosion (about 1,000 square miles).

3. Initial radiation—Extremely high dose of radiation over an area with a radius of about 2¼ miles from the point of explosion (about 15 square miles). ·

4. Residual radiation—High dose rates of radiation from fallout over an area 20–30 miles wide and 150–200 miles long, down wind from the point of explosion (3,000–6,000 square miles). The pattern of fallout and its dimensions would depend upon wind conditions at the time. It is the long-distance threat of fallout that could make it of greater danger to more people than the other effects of a nuclear explosion. If the enemy did what our military planners estimate they could do, hundreds of bombs on the United States could create hundreds of lethal ribbons of fallout. No one can say where these bombs will be dropped, nor just how the winds will effect the fallout on a particular day. It is for this reason that shelters in every community must be provided in order to save the lives of millions of people who might otherwise die from an overdose of radiation caused by fallout. Be assured, however, that even in a nuclear war, radioactive fallout will not cover the entire world and kill everything.

Although radioactive fallout is a complex subject, it is not necessary to understand the subject in great detail to be able to appreciate the danger and devise protective measures for it. The first step is answering the question: What is fallout?

When a nuclear weapon is exploded close to the ground, thousands of tons of earth and debris are forced up into the atomic cloud—a cloud which may reach an altitude of 16 miles or more before leveling off. The particles of dirt and debris become contaminated with radioactive materials from the explosion. They are scattered by the winds, especially at high altitudes, and later fall to earth in the form of dust-like particles carrying radioactive materials. This is fallout. The radiation from the fallout particles can damage living cells, causing injury or even death.

The fallout *particles* that transmit this threat to life may be visible in the form of dust, especially if fallout arrives in dangerous amounts. However, the *radiation* from the particles is invisible and can be detected and measured only through the use of special instruments.

Another important characteristic of fallout is that things, or people, who are exposed to radiation do not themselves become radioactive. Nothing that fallout contacts will become radioactive. Take the fallout away by washing an object, then there is no radiation from that object. The practical application of this fact is in the use of foods; canned foods, for example, which may be covered with radioactive dust can safely be eaten if the dust is carefully washed off the can before opening.

Protective Measures

The most important health rule concerning radioactive fallout involves a type of preventive medicine: Protect yourself from the radiation. There are three means by which the intensity of radiation is reduced and protection is achieved:

1. Time
2. Distance
3. Shielding

Time.—Although there is no way of actually destroying radioactivity, fallout radiation decreases in time through a process known as radioactive decay. This decay is rapid at first, and then becomes slower as time passes. A significant decrease in radioactivity comes during the first 24 hours of its existence. For example, if the radiation is measured as 3,000 roentgens per hour at one hour after the explosion, it would decline to 300 roentgens per hour after seven hours, and down to 30 roentgens per hour after two days. This decay rate follows the rule of thumb that every sevenfold increase of time after detonation will reduce radiation intensity by a factor of 10. Following a nuclear attack, the period of greatest danger from fallout probably would be the first 48 hours. During this high-danger period it would be essential to remain inside a good fallout shelter. After that you could probably leave the shelter for *brief* periods, but it might be several days or weeks before you and others in your community could safely spend much time in the open.

Distance.—Distance from the source of the radiation also is an important factor. For example, if a person were standing in a large, smooth field contaminated by radioactive fallout, and another person were on a tower 20 feet above the field, the radiation hazard faced by the person on the tower would be only about two-thirds of the hazard faced by the person standing on the contaminated ground. A combination of distance and shielding can provide effective fallout protection.

For example, the intermediate floors of tall buildings that are constructed of heavy materials can provide excellent fallout protection. The distance from the ground and from the roof of the building, where fallout particles would land, would provide part of the protection, and the shielding inherent in the heavy materials used in the construction of the building would provide part of the protection.

Shielding.—Shielding means shelter. Because of the high penetrating power of fallout radiation, heavy and dense materials such as dirt, stone, and concrete, are needed to absorb the damaging rays. The general rule is: The heavier or more massive your shield, the better your protection. Interior areas of large buildings offer good protection; while attic space, for instance, in a house with a wooden or asphalt shingle roof offers very little.

The Federal Government is surveying buildings throughout the Nation in order to mark those which offer good protection from fallout. These are stocked with austere supplies of water, food, medical needs, radiological instruments and sanitation equipment. The objective is to develop fallout shelter space for every person in the United States as quickly as possible. Many millions of spaces, however, will have to be provided by private industry, institutions, churches and home owners. As these public shelters are located and marked, learn where they are, and be ready to get into one quickly, if necessary. Keep informed as to whether essential supplies have been stocked or whether occupants need to bring food and water, or other items with them. This information can be obtained from your local civil defense office.

Many families in the Nation, who are too far away from public shelters, will need to build one in their own home or on their premises. The shelter area should have enough space and be stocked with enough water, food, and other essentials, to take care of your family for two weeks.

In arranging your shelter, you can provide for sleeping with tiered bunk beds, fold-up cots, or studio couches in order to save as much space as possible and provide more room during the day. If it is impossible to provide sleeping space for all, you may have to take turns in resting, some members of the family sleeping by day and others by night. One member of the group should be awake at all times to guard against bad air conditions and fire.

Privacy will be hard to achieve, but it may seem very valuable to you. Light-weight screens, easily moved and not too space-consuming, might be used to divide some of the sleeping, bathing, and sanitation areas. This is particularly desirable in apartment house or other group shelters. Curtains, hung from the ceiling or between tall pieces of furniture, could be used to provide privacy for temporary emergency toilet facilities.

You should try to arrange to have a regular electrical outlet in the shelter as power may continue in many areas covered with fallout. Candles, kerosene lamps, and other fuel-burning appliances should be used inside a shelter only when absolutely necessary. They not only use oxygen, but also give off heat and possible carbon monoxide. If electrical power fails, there should be arrangements for some type of battery-powered, low-level lighting, also a portable radio to be used to listen to emergency broadcasts. More specific details can be obtained from pamphlets you can request from your local civil defense office.

Shelter living would be crowded. You would probably face problems of temperature, ventilation, humidity, and other discomforts. Nevertheless, shelter occupancy tests have shown that typical Americans of both sexes and widely divergent ages can live under shelter conditions for periods up to two weeks without too much stress. Neither the crowding nor lack of privacy prove to be as serious a discomfort factor in shelter living as people expect them to be. Agitation and tension can be expected to be greatest immediately following shelter entry and prior to anticipated release, but can be minimized through effective planning.

The simplest activity of everyday life would require effective management in a shelter. Eating, cleaning, sleeping, personal cleanliness, sanitation, and filling time involve shelter management, adjustment, and teamwork. Arrangements for sleep, involving quiet, lighting, and conversion and relocation of bunks for night and daytime use, are very important. They would affect the sleep obtained by shelter occupants, and would be an important factor in the adequacy of shelter space.

Points to remember about protective measures against radioactive fallout:

1. The least that a person should do is to go quickly inside the best available shelter or his home, and stay there.

2. The more dirt, stone or concrete that surrounds you, the better protection you get.

3. Interior offices and space away from outside walls and roofs of tall buildings can provide good shelter.

4. All marked and stocked shelter space offers good protection.

5. Learn where these public shelters are, and if not within walking distance, build a home shelter.

6. Plans for various home shelters can be obtained from your Civil Defense Office.

7. Based upon a system of radiological measurements, levels of fallout radiation can be reported over the radio. Remain in your shelter until you know it is safe to leave.

8. Clothing will keep most radioactive dust from contact with the body, but should be removed or brushed off before entering a shelter.

POSSIBLE EFFECTS ON HUMANS

Much has been written about the possible long-range effects from exposure to radiation—increased incidence of leukemia shortening of the life span, and genetic implications. No doubt exposure to fallout radiation would result in some increases in the small percentage of such occurrences normally expected. However, other effects of radiation, called *acute* effects, could result in sickness or death in a relatively short time. In the event of a nuclear attack on the United States, it is these acute effects that would have to be dealt with first.

Although scientists generally agree on the amount of radiation damage the body can sustain without causing sickness or death, there are so many variables involved that no one can state precisely how radiation would affect all persons. For any individual case, these variables include the duration of the exposure, the age, and general health and vigor of the person. However, in spite of these and other variables, certain guidelines can be given and these are outlined in the following table:

Probable Acute Effects of Radiation

Short-term, whole body exposure in roentgens *	Probable effect
0–100	No obvious effects.
100–200	Minor incapacitations. Possibly 5 percent would require medical care.
200–400	Sickness and some deaths, but more than 50 percent would survive.
400–600	Severe sickness. Less than 50 percent would survive.
Over 600	Few survivors.

*Short-term exposure is usually defined as the total exposure over a period of about four days. A roentgen (r) is the unit used to measure exposure dose of gamma radiation. Exposure dose rate is expressed in roentgens per hour (r/hr).

These acute effects would be modified considerably if the radiation dose were received over a long period of time. The body repairs some of the damage (perhaps up to 90 percent) if it is given time. For example, a whole body exposure of 600 r or more in a short period of time—say, 4 days or less—would be fatal in most instances. But the same total exposure probably would not cause death or any noticeable effects if it were acquired in small doses over a much longer period—say, a year or more. However, it is well to keep in mind that any radiation received, other than that received for medical diagnosis and treatment, is harmful because the body can never repair all the damage. (See *Radiation Sickness* for a discussion of the symptoms of radiation sickness and the recommended treatment.)

The above figures are useful primarily for planning purposes and to civil defense officials who possess the radiological instruments and who know how to use them and interpret their readings. In the event of a nuclear attack, most people will not know even approximately the number of roentgens, if any, to which they individually have been exposed. Only those who go into an adequate shelter before fallout arrives, and remain there, can have an assurance of escaping radiation sickness.

Civil defense personnel who have emergency assignments will wear dosimeters, an instrument which will show the accumulated amount of radiation to which they may be exposed. Your local radio station will broadcast information after the attack where fallout is occurring. This is based upon reports by the civil defense radiological monitoring system. These reports are necessarily general; so, without certain knowledge of amounts of exposure to yourself, play it safe—go into shelter early and remain there.

Radiation sickness.—Like so many other sicknesses, can be treated. Depending upon the dose received, recovery is possible. Points to remember about possible radiation affects on humans:

1. People do not all react the same to equal amounts of radiation, but for most people there will be no obvious effects even to whole-body exposure of 100 roentgens. There may be, however, some harmful long-term effects.

2. With an increase in dosage over 100 roentgens whole-body exposure, people become ill.

3. A dose of 700 roentgens received in a few days with whole-body exposure will kill most people.

4. Without a certain knowledge of amounts of exposure, play it safe—go into shelter early and remain there.

5. If you have been exposed, seek the best shelter and avoid additional radiation.

6. In caring for a person suspected of radiation sickness, just be sure he is free of any fallout dust. He cannot transmit radiation sickness to you.

7. Some radiation may cause temporary sterility, or temporary loss of hair.

HEALTHFUL LIVING IN EMERGENCIES

PUBLIC FALLOUT SHELTER

This is the official fallout shelter sign of the Office of Civil Defense, Department of Defense. Look for these in your city and remember where they are, so if necessary you can go quickly to the shelter nearest you. The Federal government is provisioning public shelters with austere supplies of water and food for as many people as the shelter will hold—3½ gallons per shelter space. Survival biscuits and a carbohydrate supplement are stocked to provide 10,000 calories per shelter space. Also included are sanitation supplies, medical kits and radiological monitoring equipment. In many places local governments are stocking additional desirable items. It would be advisable to keep informed on the progress and plans in your own community concerning what things to bring to a public shelter. You would likely be requested to carry into the shelter with you such things as special foods and supplies for the baby, special dietary requirements, and other personal medical needs. Some of the items which you may not be allowed to bring with you include perishable foods, firearms, intoxicants, pets and bulky possessions. If shelter living is forced upon us by an attack or natural disaster, a great majority of the population will resort to the public shelters. Others will have their own private family shelter, and the principles of healthful living apply equally to both. If you are to have your own shelter, there are certain emergency supplies that you should have stored, and certain basic sanitation procedures you should be prepared to follow.

WATER

Water would be one of your most essential supply items in an emergency. You can get along without food for quite a while, but you must have safe drinking water. Amounts needed will vary depending upon shelter temperatures, kinds of food, and health of shelter occupants. While people can usually survive on an average of one (1) quart per person per day for drinking, it would be better to have two (2) quarts or more per person per day for food preparation and cleansing. Plan your emergency water supply for a minimum of fourteen (14) days. When there is a limited amount of water available, FIRST—set aside an adequate amount for drinking; SECOND—if anybody is suspected of having radioactive fallout on his skin, wash with soap and water; THIRD—the next most important use of water is for washing hands.

If your regular water supply comes from a community waterworks, you will have to have an emergency supply of water because the waterworks system might be affected by bomb damage, power failure, or contamination.

Glass jugs with tight-fitting covers or stoppers make good water storage containers, provided they have been thoroughly washed with soap and water and rinsed several times before being filled and sealed. They should be packed tightly with wadded newspapers or cloths between jars to prevent breakage. Polyethylene containers also are good for storing water.

Water that has been carefully stored for long periods of time will be as safe to drink as fresh water, but may not taste "fresh". Some may want to test their stored water for smell, taste every 3 months, but it is not necessary for health. Odorous as it might become, it will still be usable in an emergency.

You will also probably have available several sources of drinking water in the water system built into your house; for example, from the storage tank of a hot water heater, the flush tank of a toilet, and the house water pipes.

A well and pump is a desirable emergency source of water for drinking, food preparation, sanitation, and cooling purposes, particularly for large shelters.

Although some waterworks may be shut down after an attack, many other water plants would continue to function and to produce safe drinking water. Local authorities would let you know as soon as possible whether the public water facilities are in operation and whether the water is safe to drink.

If the public water supply is contaminated or if there is damage to the community water system, you may receive instructions to close the water shutoff valve for your house to prevent contaminated outside water from flowing and mixing with the safe water inside. Thus, it is important for you to know the location of the water shutoff valve for your house, and to make sure now that it is in good working order.

In the event of attack, use the water within the shelter first and make it last as long as possible. Do not leave the shelter during the first few days to go to other parts of the house to obtain water supplies unless it is absolutely necessary, and when you do go, collect the water rapidly so that your time outside the shelter is as short as possible.

How To Purify Water

After you have used up all your supplies of water within the house, you may have to purify water obtained from other sources. *Never use outside water without purifying it unless your local authorities say it is safe to do so.*

There are two kinds of contamination—germs and radioactive materials—which may exist in water and make it dangerous to use. They may occur separately or together. Use methods suggested below to purify water.

If the water is not clear.—Strain it through a paper towel or several layers of clean cloth to remove as much of the foreign matter as possible, or place the water in a deep container and let it settle. Then pour or siphon off the clearest part through a clean cloth or paper towel. Straining cloudy water is an important and basic step in the process of removing both germs and radioactive contamination.

To kill germs in water.—Several methods of treatment can be used. None of the following methods, however, will remove radioactive contamination from water.

1. *Water purification tablets.*—These tablets, containing iodine or chlorine, can be bought at a sporting goods store, chemical or drug store, or from a store that sells equipment for swimming pools. The bottle containing the tablets will give instructions on how to use them.

2. *Chlorination.*—Water can also be purified by chlorinating it with a household bleach solution. Make sure that the bleach you buy for this purpose is a liquid bleach of the *sodium hypochlorite type.* Labels of many such household bleaches include instructions on how to use them to purify water.

If the label does not carry any instructions for purifying water, use about 10 drops of bleach to a gallon of water.

Mix the water and bleach solution thoroughly and let it stand for 30 minutes. After that time you should still be able to smell a slight chlorine odor. This odor shows that the water is safe to use. If there is no smell of chlorine, you should again treat the water with the same amount of bleach solution as before and let it stand for another 15 minutes before you use it. *The taste or smell of chlorine in water is a sign of safety. It is not harmful. If you cannot detect chlorine by this method, do not drink the water. The bleach solution may have become too weak.*

3. *Iodine.*—Ordinary tincture of iodine may be used to purify small quantities of water. Add 20 drops to each gallon of clear water or 40 drops for cloudy water. Mix and allow to stand for 30 minutes before using.

4. *Boiling.*—If heat is available, boiling the water is a good way to destroy germs. Boil vigorously for at least one minute. To improve the taste of water after boiling, pour it back and forth from one clean container to another after it has cooled. This puts air into the water and makes it taste better.

To remove radioactive contamination from water.—As pointed out earlier, although boiling or the chemical treatments will kill harmful germs, they will not remove radioactive contamination from water. If such contamination exists, your local authorities will advise you.

Surface water supplies, such as rivers, lakes, and open reservoirs may be contaminated by fallout. However, many fallout particles are so heavy that they quickly settle to the bottom. Also, the regular water treatment (coagulation, sedimentation, filtration) of public water systems will remove most of the fallout contamination. Very little of the dangerous fallout material would be dissolved in the water.

Water softener or ion exchange systems used in many buildings and homes will remove most of what little fallout may be dissolved in the water in the same manner as is done to chemicals which cause "hard" water.

It should not be necessary to purify the water you have stored in closed containers.

FOOD

You should have at least a 2-week supply of food on hand at all times. Include foods that fit the habits and preferences of your family, that will provide a balanced diet, and are rich in energy. Avoid heavily salted foods because they will increase your need for drinking water.

For diabetics, babies, and others needing special diets, you should store an adequate supply of the proper foods.

You will need foods that do not require refrigeration because your gas or electricity may be shut off. The major portion of your food supply should be made up of foods not needing cooking. Shelter cooking would be improvised at best, and difficult. Also, any open flame will use up oxygen, liberate heat, and may produce carbon monoxide.

Some Suggested Foods

Canned.—Fish; Fruit and Juices—these will help supply your liquid requirements; Macaroni; Meats; Milk—particularly if there are babies, invalids, or old people; Poultry; Soups; Spaghetti; Stews; Vegetables.

Packaged.—Candy; Cereals, some sugared; Cookies; Crackers; Raisins.

Also.—Bouillon cubes; Coffee, Tea, instant type; Cooking fats and oils; Cheese spreads; Honey; Jam; Peanut butter; Salt; Sugar.

Food required for special diets.

Baby food—Strained Meats, Fruits, and Vegetables.

You should use foods from your emergency supply regularly, and replace them.

Making Sure Stored Food Is Safe

After an enemy attack, the contents of cans, jars, cartons, and other food packages that have not been broken would be safe to eat. Food that has been stored indoors should be safe to eat. Wipe or wash carefully cans, bottles, or other containers that may have been covered by radioactive dust. Contaminated fresh fruits or vegetables should be prepared for eating as described under "Contamination Precautions." Dispose of the rags or water and contaminated fruit peelings by placing these outside the shelter.

Refrigerators and home freezers should be kept closed as much as possible, especially if gas and electricity are cut off, to conserve perishable food. If the gas or electric service is not restored within 12 hours, eat or cook the most perishable items. If they begin to spoil, throw them away before they contaminate other foods that keep better.

Food will keep in home freezer units for varying periods after the power is shut off. If the capacity of the freezer is 4 cubic feet, the food in it will keep about 3 days; if the capacity is 12–36 cubic feet, the food will keep about 5 days.

Fresh milk sours easily, and nonrefrigerated milk should be used as rapidly as possible. However, sour milk is not harmful to health.

EMERGENCY SANITATION

Good sanitation procedures are always an important part of maintaining good health, and they would be particulary important in the emergency period following a nuclear attack. Following is some basic information on supplies you should have and procedures you should follow in an emergency.

Sanitation Supplies

Detergent; Soap—also needed in caring for sickness or injury (See "Medical and First Aid Supplies.") ; Water purification tablets (iodine or chlorine) ; tincture of iodine or household bleach may also be used; Pail with cover—small size to use as temporary toilet; Cans with tight covers for storing wastes; Cans with tight covers for garbage; Old newspapers; Rubbish box; Plastic bags; Household bleach to use as disinfectant; Creosol (saponated cresol solution) ; Insecticides; Rubber pants and disposable diapers (if needed, for babies) ; Rubber sheeting; Sanitary napkins—also useful as dressings (See "Medical and First Aid Supplies.") ; Toilet tissue.

Disposal of Sewage

Failure to dispose properly of human wastes can lead to the spread of such diseases as typhoid, dysentery, and diarrhea.

If water service is interrupted by a nuclear attack, you will not be able to use a water flush toilet, and one of your first tasks to make shelter living possible and safe will be to provide temporary toilet facilities.

As indicated under "Sanitation Supplies," a metal pail with a cover can be used as a temporary emergency toilet. A commode, such as is often used in the bedroom of invalids and elderly persons, would probably provide a more comfortable arrangement. You can improvise a commode by cutting out the seat in a chair and placing a pail under it. A plastic bag placed in the pail with the bag top overlapping the seat will be helpful in confining wastes and in waste disposal. A household disinfectant, such as creosol, may help to control odors if a small amount is put in the toilet after each use.

The contents of the emergency toilet should be emptied into a second larger can (a covered garbage can or other waterproof container) as often as necessary for storage. The larger storage can should be placed as far away from the people in the shelter as possible and kept tightly closed. A supply of old newspapers—at least a week's accumulation—will come in handy for various sanitary uses, such as wrapping garbage and lining large containers.

When radioactive fallout no longer presents a severe hazard, the wastes that you have accumulated should be removed from the shelter area, taken outside, and buried under 12 to 24 inches of earth. Never deposit wastes, liquid or solid, on the surface of the ground. Insects and rodents may carry infection from them to humans. In urban areas, local authorities may make arrangements to collect and dispose of wastes.

Disinfectants (household bleach and creosol) may be helpful in controlling odors. They will also help control insect breeding in containers that cannot be emptied immediately. Store such disinfectants safely away from children in the shelter.

If there is chronic illness in the family that requires rubber sheeting or other special sanitary equipment, make sure now that adequate supplies are available.

If there is a baby in your shelter, you may find diaper laundering a problem under disaster conditions. It is best to keep on hand an ample supply of disposable diapers. However, if these are not available, emergency diaper needs can be met by lining rubber pants with cleansing tissue, toilet paper, scraps of cloth, or other absorbent materials. If you prefer, any moisture-resistant material can be cut and folded to diaper size and lined with absorbent material.

Disposal of Garbage and Rubbish

Garbage sours and decomposes. It must be properly stored and handled if odor and insect nuisances are to be prevented in the shelter.

Wrap the garbage in several thicknesses of newspaper before putting it into your garbage container. The paper will absorb some of the remaining moisture and make possible longer storage without unpleasant odors. A tight-fitting lid on the garbage can is important to keep odors in, and flies and other insects out.

When radioactive fallout no longer presents a severe hazard, garbage may be disposed of outside the shelter in the same manner as human wastes.

Rubbish should be kept at a minimum and placed in a large container, separate from garbage. When it is safe to take it outside, it may be burned.

Vermin Control

Control of vermin would be an important factor in disease control following an enemy attack. There are actions that can be taken now, and procedures to follow during an emergency that would be effective.

Preparedness Action.—Keeping vermin under control *now* would lessen the health danger from insects and rodents during an emergency period. This involves good sanitation habits, including the sanitary disposal of human wastes, garbage, and rubbish, and the use of pesticides when necessary.

Spraying or painting the interior of the family fallout shelter with a 5 percent DDT solution is a good preparedness action for insect control. The insecticide will be effective for several months if it is applied to the walls and ceiling of the shelter to the point of obvious dampness. Insecticides containing chlordane, dieldrin, diazinon, malathion, or ronnel also may be used for this purpose. In using these insecticides, extreme care should be exercised to avoid inhalation or contact with the skin. Should accidental contact occur, the affected skin areas should be washed immediately with soap and water.

In addition, you should have quick-acting insecticides which rely on pyrethrum or pyrethrins (available at most grocery stores), a fly swatter, and screening material ready for use in an emergency, and mouse and rat traps, particularly if rodents are a problem in your area.

Emergency Procedures.—Previously described emergency procedures for the sanitary disposal of sewage, garbage, and rubbish would be an essential part of vermin control following an enemy attack. In addition, the use of screening to keep out insects, and insecticides to kill them would be important. For safety purposes in a crowded shelter, and also for quick action, insecticides containing pyrethrum as the principal active ingredient are most useful.

For the control of lice or other insects infesting the body, a 10 percent DDT dust or a 1 percent lindane dust is recommended. The dust should remain on the body, in hairy places, and in the clothing for at least 24 hours, and then be washed off. A second treatment 7 to 10 days later will kill lice that have hatched since the first treatment.

Traps and clubs may be the best way to kill mice and rats in the confined area of a fallout shelter. Poisons, such as warfarin, should prove effective, but take time to act on rodents so are useful only in the general area outside the shelter proper.

Special precautions should be taken in storing and using poisons to make sure that they are out of the reach of children. It would be dangerous to use poison baits *inside* a fallout shelter. Also, insecticides in spray form should be used with great care in the closed, confined area of a shelter. Inhalation of their fumes could be dangerous, an explosive hazard is possible, and the spray could injure the eyes of those in the shelter. Dusts and wettable powders are safer to use than sprays in a closed area. Be sure to observe the precautions given on the label when using any insecticide or other poison.

Contamination Precautions

If there is falling fine ash or dust, you may have been exposed to fallout before reaching shelter. Shake your clothing outside the shelter before entering it. Once inside, wipe off or preferably wash your body and hair if water is available. Also clean off any supplies you are carrying which may have been similarly contaminated. If there is a drain in the shelter, pour this wash water down it. Otherwise throw the water and wiping materials outside.

Obviously, you should not leave a shelter while fallout is still coming down. And you should not leave it later, unless vital to do so, without being informed by local authorities that it is safe to do so, or without measuring the intensity of the radiation in your area with a special instrument. (Radiation measuring instruments, developed for use by the public, are available. Local civil defense authorities can give you information about the instruments.)

At first you may be able to stay outside the shelter only for brief periods, but as radioactivity decreases, the time outside can be lengthened. The radiation hazard decreases rapidly in the early period after the burst. During the first 48 hours, fallout radiation may decrease to about 5 percent or less of its original intensity. Even at the end of two weeks, however, plants and objects which have received considerable fallout may still be dangerous. Even if your local authorities report it safe for you to leave your shelter and move about outside, the fruits and vegetables you may gather from a garden should be cleaned before you eat them.

You should take the following steps:

1. If the fruits or vegetables are of good size and solid (like beets, peaches, or potatoes) *first wash* them carefully and *then peel* them.

2. If they are covered with a husk or with outer leaves (like corn, head lettuce, or cabbage) *remove* the husk or leaves *first*, then wash the inner contents.

3. If it is a vegetable or fruit (like spinach or strawberries) which can neither be peeled nor husked, *do not eat it* unless food is scarce. In any case, wash such foods thoroughly before using.

Do not attempt to add to your water supply from containers that have caught rainwater running off a contaminated roof.

When you leave the shelter, you should wear heavy shoes, or rubbers or boots over your regular shoes. It would also be desirable to wear coveralls over the clothes you wear in the shelter. Gloves should be worn if you are going to handle anything that might be contaminated.

These outer coverings should be removed upon your return, just outside the entrance to your shelter. If any part of your body has been contaminated by the radioactive dust, brush it off before reentering the shelter, and wash with soap and water, if possible. Then dispose of the water.

Household pets will be subject to the same radiation dangers as humans and should be treated accordingly. Pets should not be permitted to go outside and then reenter the shelter until it is known that there is no longer a radiation hazard in the area. Otherwise, they could bring in considerable amounts of radioactive particles.

If you plan to keep a pet with you in your shelter, you will need a supply of food and water for him, and you must be careful to dispose of animal wastes in as sanitary a fashion as you do human.

SECTION II

ARTIFICIAL RESPIRATION

What To Do

MOUTH-TO-MOUTH METHOD

1. Place the person who has stopped breathing on his back.
2. Clear the mouth and throat completely to insure an open airway to the lungs.

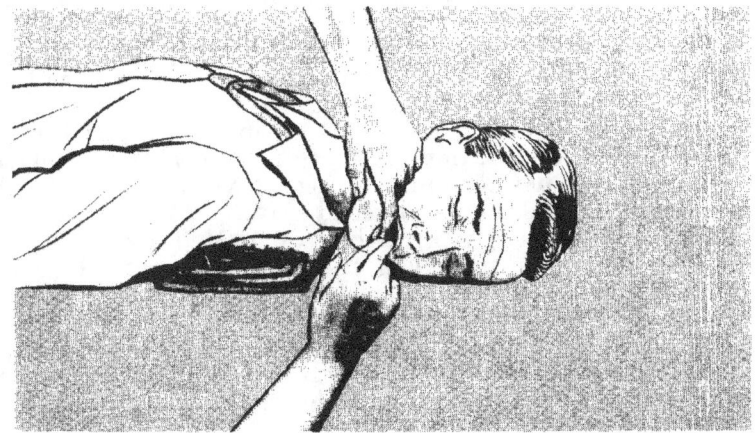

3. Tilt his head back so that his chin points upward and lift his lower jaw from beneath and behind so that it juts out.
4. START ARTIFICIAL RESPIRATION IMMEDIATELY. The most important lifesaving action is to get air into the person's lungs quickly.

If some injury prohibits the use of the mouth-to-mouth, use the:

BACK-PRESSURE ARM-LIFT METHOD

1. Place person who has stopped breathing in position shown below.

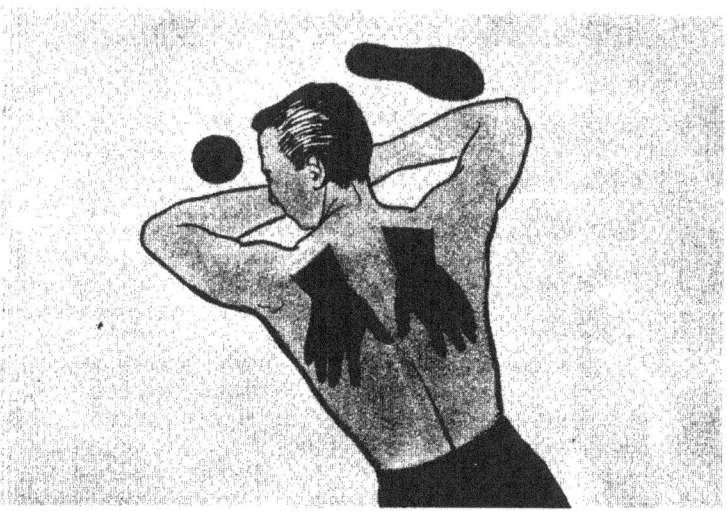

2. Clear mouth and throat.
3. Start artificial respiration immediately.

An adult at rest breathes about 18 times a minute, taking in about a pint of air with each breath.

Breathing may stop as a result of gas or drug poisoning, electric shock, choking, drowning, suffocation, injuries to the head, neck, or chest, poliomyelitis, or convulsions.

Most persons can live only about 6 minutes after breathing stops. Artificial respiration must begin as soon as possible after natural breathing has been interrupted or when natural breathing is so irregular or shallow as to be ineffective.

Artificial respiration is a method of getting air into and out of a person's lungs until he can breathe for himself. It is a life-saving measure.

One of the simplest and most effective ways to give artificial respiration is by the mouth-to-mouth (or mouth-to-nose) method. This method is effective for both children and adults and can be used even when there are injuries to the chest and arms.

Here is how to do it:

1. Place the person who has stopped breathing on his back.
2. Open his mouth and clear out any foreign matter such as food or dirt, with your fingers or a cloth wrapped around your fingers. If the person has false teeth, remove them.
3. Tilt his head back so that his chin points upward and lift his lower jaw from beneath and behind so that it juts out. This

moves the base of the tongue away from the back of the throat, so it does not block the air passage to the lungs. *Unless this air passage is open, no amount of effort will get air in.*

4. You can blow air into a person's lungs through either his mouth or nose. Open your mouth wide and place it tightly over the person's mouth. Pinch his nostrils shut. *Or* close the victim's mouth and place your mouth over his nose. *With an infant or small child, place your mouth over both his nose and mouth, making an airproof seal.* Air can be blown through an unconscious person's teeth even though they may be clenched.

5. Blow into the mouth or nose, continuing to hold the unconscious person's lower jaw so that it juts out to keep the air passage open.

6. Remove your mouth from the patient's mouth. Turn your head to the side and listen for the return outflow of air coming from the patient's lungs. If you hear it, you will know that an exchange of air has occurred.

7. You can then continue your breathing for the patient. Blow vigorously into his mouth or nose about 12 times each minute. Remove your mouth after each breath and listen for the exchange of air. In the case of an infant or child, blow less vigorously, using shallower breaths about 20 times a minute.

8. If you are not getting an exchange of air, turn the person on his side and strike him several times between the shoulder blades, using considerable force. This will help dislodge any obstruction in the air passages. Check the position of the head and jaw. Again make sure there is no foreign matter in his mouth. If you wish to avoid direct contact, you may hold a cloth (piece of gauze, handkerchief, or other material) over the victim's mouth or nose, and breathe through it. The cloth does not greatly affect the exchange of air. However, do not waste precious seconds looking for a cloth if one is not handy.

Normal breathing may sometimes start up again after 15 minutes of artificial respiration. But if it doesn't, you should continue the procedure until you are positive life is gone. Alternate with other persons, if possible, so as to maintain maximum efficiency. Cases of electric shock, and drug or carbon monoxide poisoning may require artificial respiration for long periods.

The first signs of restored breathing may be a sigh. There may be irregular breathing at first. Artificial respiration should be continued until regular breathing occurs.

When normal breathing resumes, the person usually recovers rapidly. But he should rest for several hours. Then he may gradually return to normal activities unless other injuries exist.

The back-pressure, arm-lift method of artificial respiration is the second most desirable method. It should be used only when injuries to the head or face prevent the use of the mouth-to-mouth or mouth-to-nose method.

MOUTH-TO-MOUTH AND MOUTH-TO-NOSE METHOD

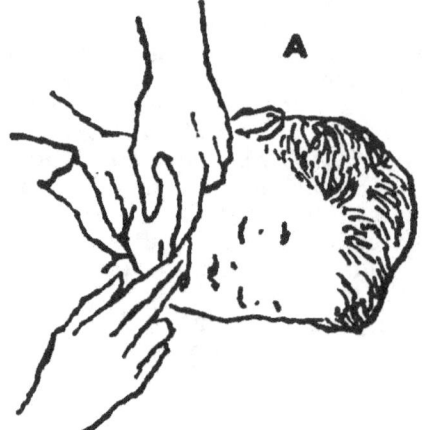

Before starting any type of artificial respiration be sure that the mouth and throat are completely clear of mucus and foreign objects. Use your fingers to clean the mouth. You may cover fingers with a piece of cloth to help remove mucus and slippery objects.

The head must be tipped back to allow a free air passage with the jaw held in a jutting out position. The more you can achieve the "sword swallower" position the better.

Remember—Don't blow too hard. Your mouth and the mouth of the person receiving treatment should be wide open with a complete seal between them. Inhale more than usual before exhaling into person's mouth. In this way he will get more oxygen.

D

Pinching the nostrils prevents air from escaping through the nose. With your right hand be sure to hold the jaw in the jutting out position. Your fingers, held like a claw, should be hooked behind the jawbone to hold it in the correct position.

E

This is the mouth-to-nose type of respiration with the lips being sealed by the two fingers of the right hand. This would be used when an obstruction is in the mouth that cannot be removed, or a severe mouth injury prevents proper contact.

BACK PRESSURE ARMLIFT METHOD

This picture shows the correct position of the knee, foot, and hands in the first step of back pressure armlift method. The knee and foot may be alternated to make it less tiring for the person administering this type of artificial respiration.

A

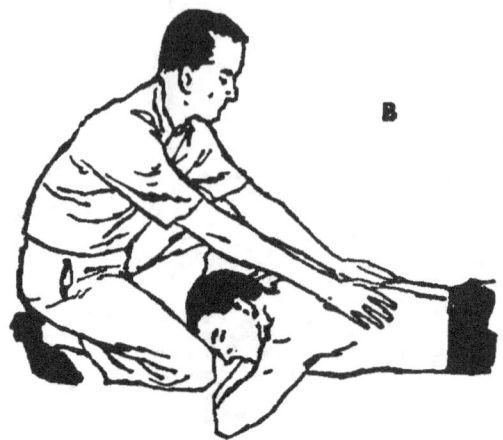

B

With hands in correct position the operator starts a rocking forward motion. Note that elbows are straight and stiff. This is when you start the timing. Chant: "Press—Release"—"Lift—Release." Say it in time to your own breathing.

With arms almost vertical direct pressure is applied to the back. *Do not* use quick, jerking pressure. Use *Smooth* even pressure. Release the pressure in the same smooth way. Pull your hands away slowly.

C

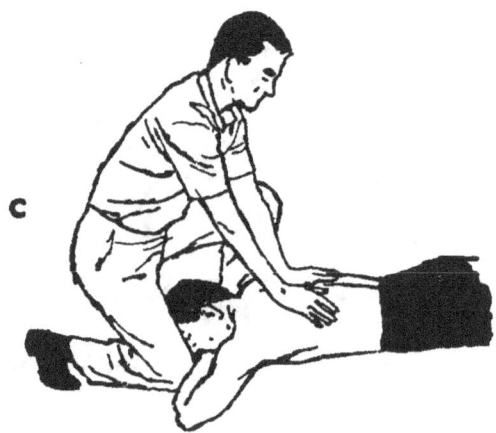

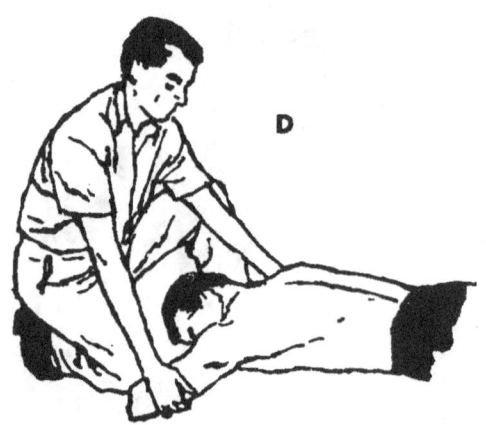

D

As the operator rocks back to his original position he grasps each arm just above the elbow. This is the next part of the timing. Chant: "Lift — Release." Slow — Regular—Even.

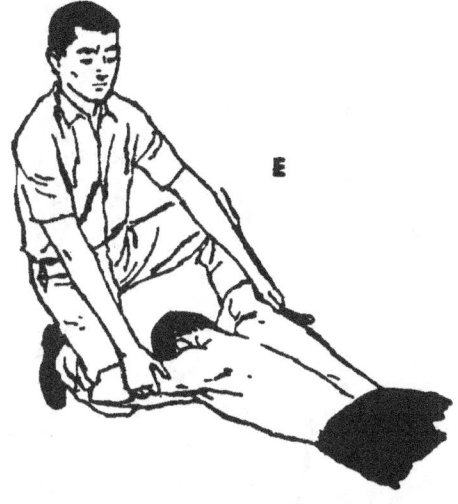

E

The operator continues to rock back lifting the arms up and toward him. This is the end of one cycle. He will next place his hands in correct position on the back and start over again.

BLEEDING AND BANDAGING

What To Do

1. Apply dressing or pad directly over wound.
2. Apply direct even pressure—use your bare hand if necessary when bleeding is serious, and dressing not immediately available.
3. Leave dressing in place.
4. Continue pressure by applying bandage.
5. Secure bandage in place—check to be sure bandage is not too tight and cutting off circulation.
6. Elevate limb above heart level except where there is a possible broken bone.
7. Treat for shock.
8. IF BLOOD SOAKS THROUGH DRESSING DO NOT remove but apply more dressings.

ATTENTION! !

Do not use a tourniquet unless it is impossible to stop excessive life-threatening bleeding by any other method.

EXCESSIVE BLEEDING

Bleeding needs immediate attention. Even the loss of small amounts of blood will produce weakness and can cause the condition known as shock. The loss of as much as a pint of blood by a child or a quart of blood by an adult may have disastrous results.

The first step in controlling bleeding is to exert direct pressure over the wound area. You can do this best by placing the cleanest

To stop bleeding apply dressing or pad directly over the wound and then apply pressure. Remember—immediate, direct pressure—even with the bare hand—is the important action to stop bleeding.

Continue the pressure until the bleeding has stopped or slowed to the point that you will be able to apply a bandage. Don't be in a hurry to stop the pressure.

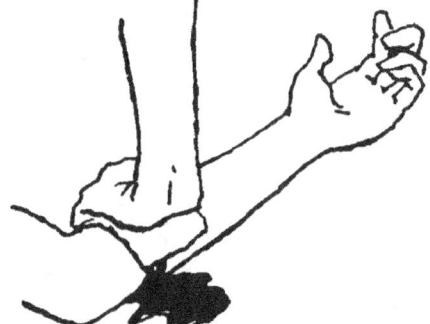

material available (a pad of sterile gauze is best) against the bleeding point, and applying firm pressure with your hand until a bandage can be applied.

The cleaner the cloth, the better in preventing infection. But if sterile gauze is not handy, use a freshly laundered handkerchief, strip torn from a sheet, a shirt, slip, or a sanitary napkin.

The pad should be large enough to overlap the edges of the wound and, if possible, the pressure should be applied in a manner that brings the edges of the wound together.

When bleeding is serious you may have to use your bare hand while waiting for someone else to get material for a dressing. This can place dangerous germs in the wound and cause infection but it is obviously better to run the risk of infection than to let the person bleed to death.

Pressure should be applied evenly over the entire area of the wound. Properly applied, pressure squeezes broken blood vessels closed and helps clots to form; these block the blood vessels and prevent further loss of blood. However, if the pressure is unevenly applied, by bearing down with more force on one area of the wound, it may cause the bleeding to persist. Continue to apply pressure evenly until the bleeding stops.

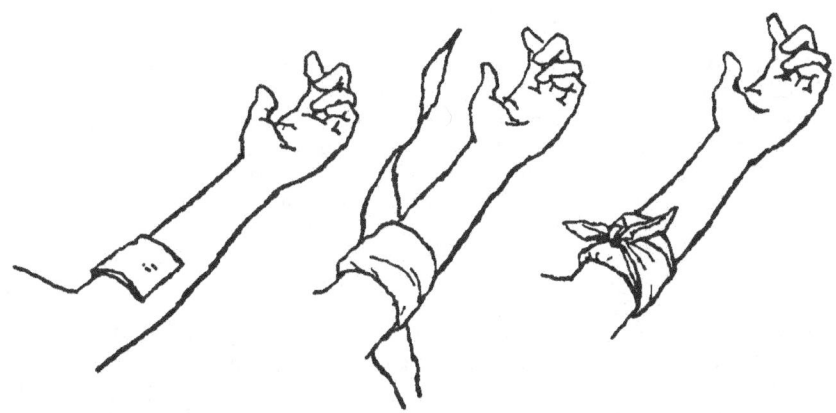

Apply the bandage firmly over the dressing to continue the pressure and thus continue to stop the bleeding. CAUTION.—Check the bandage after you have tied the knot to be sure it is not too tight and is not cutting off circulation.

After the bleeding has been controlled, do not remove the dressing from the wound, even though blood has saturated it. Simply apply additional layers of cloth to form a good-sized covering and bandage snugly and firmly. The material you place directly over the wound (the dressing) should be sterile (if available), but the material to hold the dressing in place (the bandage) need not be sterile. If roller bandage is not available, strips from a sheet or shirt will do.

After a wound stops bleeding and the bandage is firmly in place, you can turn your attention to other important needs of the patient. Anyone who has lost much blood will need treatment for shock whether or not he shows signs of shock. (See "Shock".) In addition to this care, the wound area, if on an arm or leg, should be elevated on pillows.

A bandage that is too tight can cause further injury. Because of possible swelling around the wound, check the bandage periodically and loosen it, if it seems to interfere with the circulation of the blood.

The patient should be kept warm and quiet. When his strength returns, allow him to resume normal activities gradually. At first, that means standing or walking for only 15 or 20 minutes in a morning or afternoon. Do not let him get tired.

TOURNIQUET WARNING

The application of a tourniquet to control bleeding is mentioned here principally to discourage its use. It is dangerous to apply, dangerous to leave on, dangerous to remove. It will cause tissue injury and shut off the entire blood supply to the part below, causing gangrene and loss of the limb. A tourniquet is rarely required and should be used only for severe, life-threatening hemorrhage that cannot be controlled by other means.

CARING FOR WOUNDS

Injuries that break the skin are considered "wounds." In addition to damage to the tissues at the wound edge and possible blood loss, wounds are hazards to health since germs are always on the skin and can get in through a wound and cause serious infection.

If you take proper care of wounds as soon as they occur, you will cut down the possibility of serious infection.

You should wash the skin immediately around a wound gently with water and soap or detergent, using a piece of sterile gauze or clean cloth, wiping away from the wound. Do not touch the wound with your bare fingers.

After cleaning the wound area, cover it with a sterile dressing or folded clean cloth. Fix the dressing in place with a bandage or with strips of adhesive tape. For larger wounds where it is difficult to keep a dressing in place, a triangular bandage can be used.

If there is a possibility that the bone under a wound is broken, that part of the body should be kept completely still. This will reduce the possibility of delayed bleeding, prevent further injury, promote healing, and decrease pain and discomfort. (See "Broken Bones.")

SUCKING WOUNDS IN THE CHEST

"Sucking wounds" are chest wounds in which an opening may be created from the lungs to outside air. These wounds are caused by such injuries as crushing blows or penetrating objects. Air may enter and blow out of the wound with "sucking" or hissing sounds. Froth or bubbles may be seen. Cover this opening immediately. Put your hands at each side of the wound, push together, as victim breathes out, to cover the opening. Cover the wound with a sterile dressing, holding it firmly in place while bandaging to make it airtight. Have the patient lie down but keep his shoulders slightly raised, supported with pillows. Do not attempt to lessen shock by elevating his feet if doing so makes his breathing more difficult.

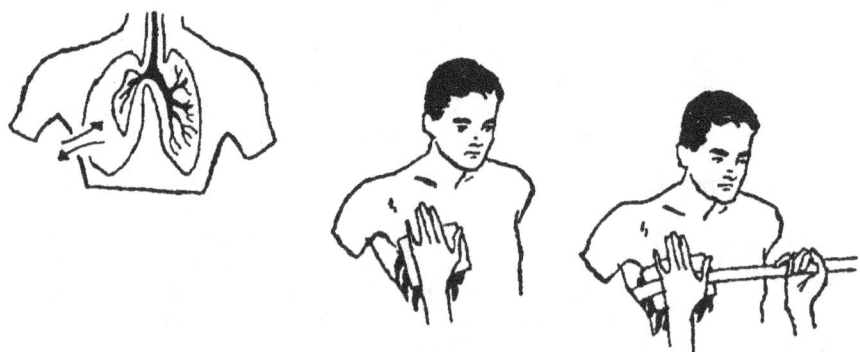

A sucking chest wound causes the lung to collapse. You must make the opening air-tight in order that the lung may continue to function properly. Place a dressing firmly over the wound and hold this pad or dressing securely in place. You must *stop* the air from passing through the wound.

INFECTION IN WOUNDS

Infection in a wound is easy to recognize. The wound will become red or discolored, swollen, painful, and at times pus will appear. The person may also appear sick and feverish. When the wound is on the arm or leg, red streaks may sometimes extend from the wound up the arm or leg and small tender lumps may appear in the armpit or groin, nearest the wound.

For the treatment of infected wounds, elevate the wound area on pillows. Keep the part at rest and apply warm packs to the wound area.

The warm packs are prepared by adding two teaspoonfuls of salt to a quart of water which has been boiled. Then cloths or towels are dipped in this solution and partially wrung out. The solution is kept warm but not so hot that it will burn the patient.

The warm packs are applied for 30 minutes and changed as often as is necessary during that time to maintain comfortable heat to the wound. These periods of warm packing are alternated with 30-minute free periods during which warm packs are not applied to the wound and it is allowed to dry.

This treatment is continued while the patient is awake and until the wound looks better. This may take several days.

The patient should be encouraged to take adequate food and fluid, eating and drinking as he wishes. Aspirin may be given for pain if necessary.

When the infection has subsided and the redness, swelling, and pus have decreased, you should still keep a sterile dressing over the wound. Dressings should be used until the wound has healed.

FRACTURES AND SPLINTING

What To Do

1. Look for bleeding and control it.
2. Whenever in doubt, treat as a fracture.
3. Apply the splint at the site of the accident.
4. Never move the person before splinting unless his life would be further in danger.
5. Prevent shock, further injury, and infection.
6. Splint securely enough to prevent any voluntary or involuntary motion at the point of fracture.
7. Check splint ties frequently to be sure it does not interfere with circulation of blood.

In most cases of severe injury there is the possibility that the person may stop breathing. If this should occur stop all other lifesaving procedures and administer artificial respiration.

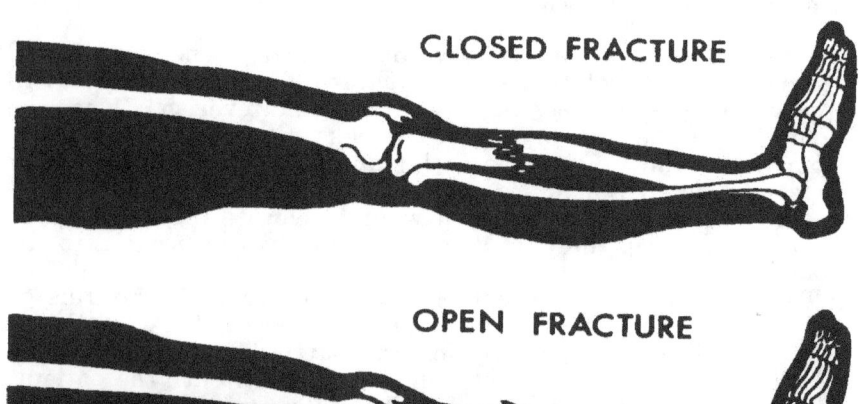

CLOSED FRACTURE

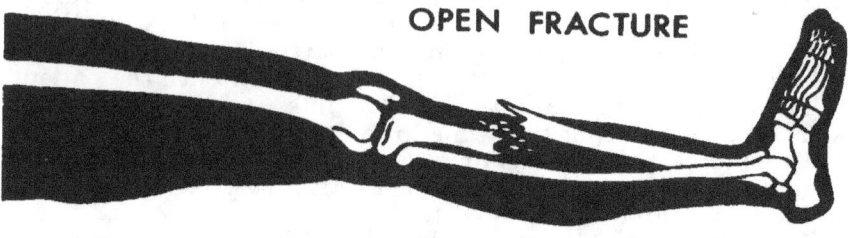

OPEN FRACTURE

The top figure is a closed fracture but with improper handling it can very easily become a fracture such as you see in the bottom picture. All fractures or suspected fractures should be handled very carefully to avoid further injury.

BROKEN BONES

Any break in a bone is called a fracture. If the ends of a broken bone do not come through the skin, the break is called a closed (or simple) fracture. If one or both ends of a broken bone come through the skin, the break is called an open (or compound) fracture. An open fracture is serious because germs can get in and cause infection.

In an open fracture, you will be able to see the wound where the bone breaks the skin. The bone itself may not be visible; it may slip back under the skin after breaking through.

In the case of a closed fracture, it is obviously more difficult to be sure that a break has occurred. One sign is pain at or near the break and tenderness and swelling around it. By running your finger gently along the bone, you may be able to feel an irregular piece of bone. A more obvious sign of a closed fracture may be the twisted or crooked unnatural position of an arm or leg or its appearance of being shorter than normal. The injured person may find it painful or impossible to move the limb.

Whenever there is any reason to believe that there may be a broken bone, treat the injury as though it actually is a fracture. Otherwise, you may cause further injury.

The important *first thing to do* is to prevent motion at the site of the break. This can be done by applying a splint to immobilize the broken bone ends. Do not move the injured person before this is done. Splint the break where he lies.

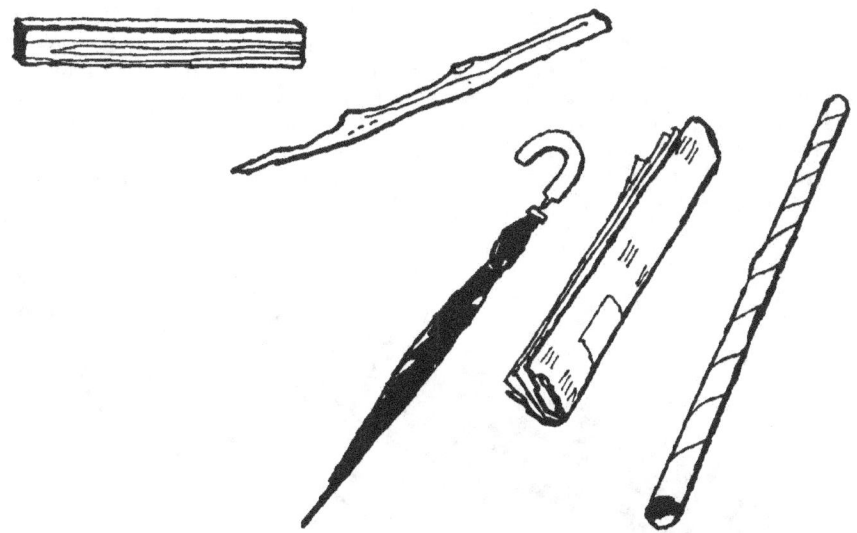

Here are just a few ideas of improvised materials to be used for splinting. Look around the room right now and see how many items you can find that could be used in the event of an emergency.

It may sometimes be necessary to straighten a limb slightly in order to apply a splint. To prevent movement of the broken bone ends while this is being done, one person should support the broken bone with his hands—one placed just above the break and one just below—while a second person grasps the end of the limb and exerts a strong steady pull to straighten it.

An exception to this preliminary immobilization of bone ends will be necessary in the case of an open fracture where a broken end of bone still sticks out of the wound. It cannot be left in that position. Allow it to slip back naturally under the skin when the limb is being straightened. Do not attempt to push it back in. Put on a sterile dressing to control bleeding and keep out germs. A clean sheet or towel can be used if necessary. Bandage the dressing in place with firm pressure. Then splint.

Splints can be made of almost any material that is rigid enough to give support to the fractured body part. They can be made of wood or metal, padded with cotton or cloth, or they can be improvised from umbrellas, tightly rolled newspapers, magazines, blankets or pillows, if necessary. In applying splints see that they extend beyond the joint above and below the fracture. Unless the joints are also immobilized in this way, they will move and disturb the broken bone.

Fasten a splint in place with bandages or strips of cloth, handkerchiefs, neckties, or belts. After splinting the limb, elevate it above the level of the heart with pillows.

Check bandage and splint fastenings at intervals to make sure that they are firm but not so tight that they cause swelling in the injured area or interfere with the circulation of blood. In doing this, do not remove the bandage from the wound because it might introduce infection or start bleeding. If the injured person complains that the arm or leg feels like it is "asleep," this may be due to a splint that is too tight. Loosen the ties which hold the splint, or, if necessary, replace the splint. This will help the "asleep" feeling unless it is caused by internal damage other than the broken bone.

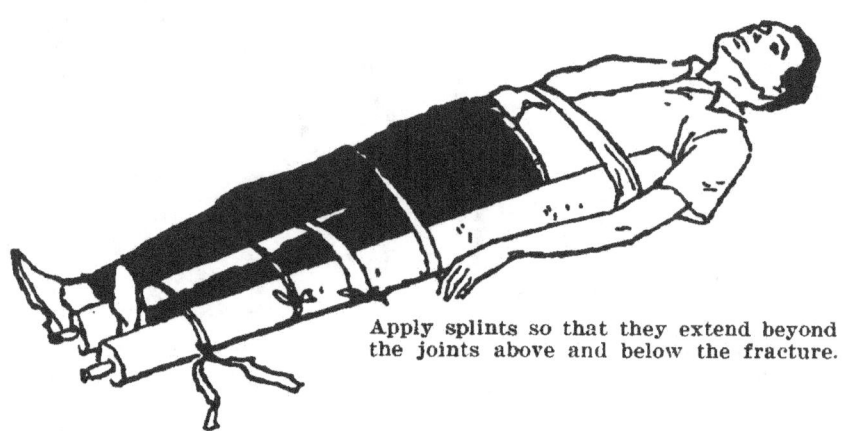

Apply splints so that they extend beyond the joints above and below the fracture.

A broken collarbone can be immobilized by putting the arm on the side of the break in a sling (made with a triangular bandage) and then binding the arm close to the body.

If a triangular bandage is not available, you can make a sling by folding a large square cloth diagonally to make a triangle. Tie the ends around the neck. Let the fingers dangle outside the edge of the sling.

A broken rib should be suspected if a chest injury is accompanied by sharp pain. The pain is usually located at the point of rib fracture and is increased markedly by the movements of the body, especially in breathing or coughing.

Swelling or deformity may sometimes be seen on thin individuals, but these signs are generally not visible.

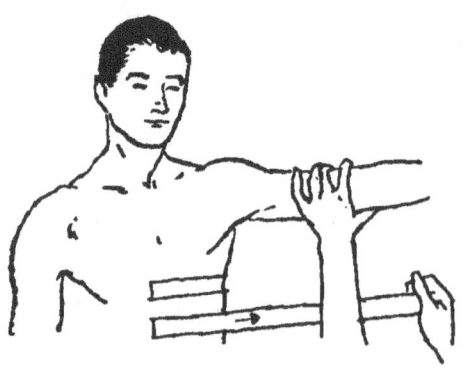

Pain may be relieved by strapping the chest with long strips of two-inch adhesive tape. Start strapping from above the point of fracture and continue down the chest wall. Apply the strips so that they extend from a point on the unfractured side of the chest (about two inches beyond the midline in the back) over the fractured side of the chest to a point on the unfractured side in front (about two inches beyond the midline.) When the strapping is finished, the adhesive strips should cover an area both above and below the tender spot.

You will be able to strap the patient's chest properly if you have him blow the air out of his lungs before you apply the adhesive strips. If you can't finish strapping him before he needs to draw another breath, stop, let him take a small breath, and exhale again. Then complete your strapping.

Fractures of the back are serious because of the danger of injury to the spinal cord. Moving a person with a back injury may cause the edges of the broken bones to cut the spinal cord, causing paralysis or death.

If it is necessary to move him, he should be placed on his back, on a stiff board or door. Keep his head, back, and legs in a straight line at all times.

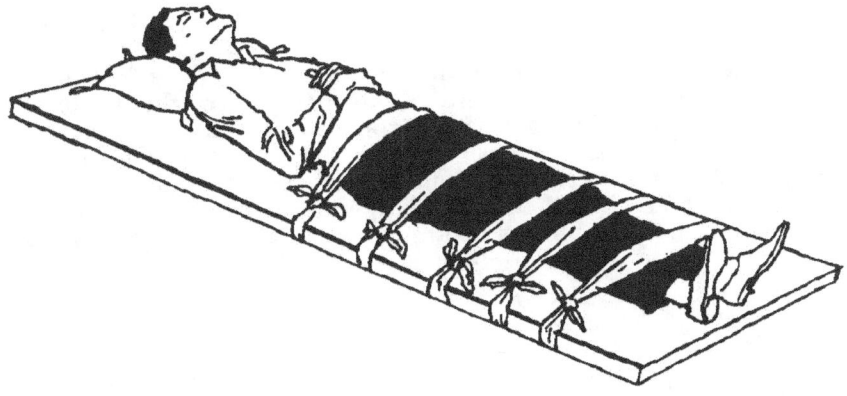

A *fractured neck* is extremely serious because of the danger to the spinal cord. It is important that the head, neck, and shoulders be maintained in the relative positions in which they are found. In moving a person with a fractured neck, it should be the duty of one person to hold the patient's head steady so that his head, neck, and shoulders can be moved as a unit without bending the neck. The patient should be transported flat on his back and should also be placed in bed flat on his back without a pillow. His head should be immobilized by placing soft but firm material such as small sandbags, on either side of his head, and he must be kept in this position.

A *fractured skull or serious head injury* may bring headache, nausea, dizziness, and unconsciousness. The person's face may be flushed and hot, his breathing slow and noisy. There may be bleeding from the nose, ears, or mouth. There may be partial paralysis and signs of shock.

In such a case, keep the person lying down, with his head and shoulders slightly raised if his face is flushed. Control visible bleeding from scalp, face, or forehead by pressure dressings.

In all cases of fracture or suspected fracture of any body part, the patient should be treated for shock.

It may sometimes be necessary to straighten a limb slightly in order to apply a splint. To prevent movement of the broken bone ends while this is being done, one person should support the broken limb with his hands. One hand placed just above the break and one just below, while a second person grasps the end of the limb and exerts a strong, steady pull to straighten it.

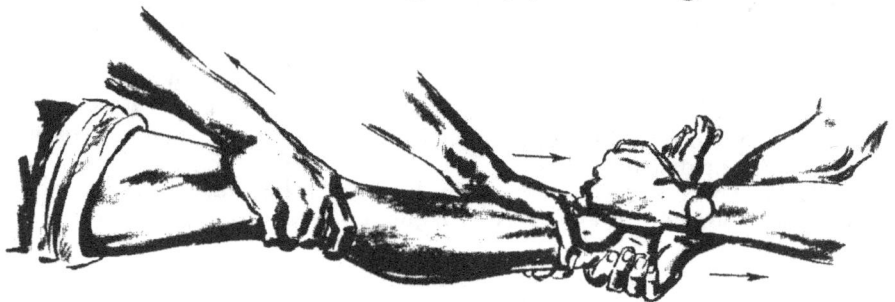

An exception to this preliminary immobilization of bone ends will be necessary in the case of an open fracture where a broken end of bone still sticks out of the wound is that it cannot be left in that position. Before straightening the limb and allowing the bone to slip back under the skin, the bone end should be carefully checked but not handled. If it appears to be dirty (street dirt, floor dirt, earth, or human or animal excreta) it should be rinsed.

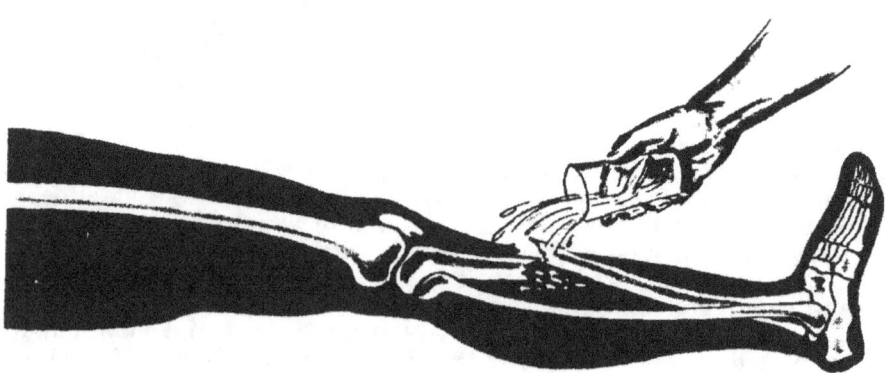

Do not handle the bone with your hands. A one (1%) percent saline solution (1 teaspoonful of salt to 1 quart of water) should be used to rinse the area as shown above. Use sterile (boiled) water if possible; if not, use safe warm drinking water, then while bone end is still wet, traction may be applied sufficient to let the bone end slip back under the skin and be in approximate alignment.

Other than the necessity described above *do not* attempt to set or reduce a fracture, you may cause severe damage to the inside of the fractured limb.

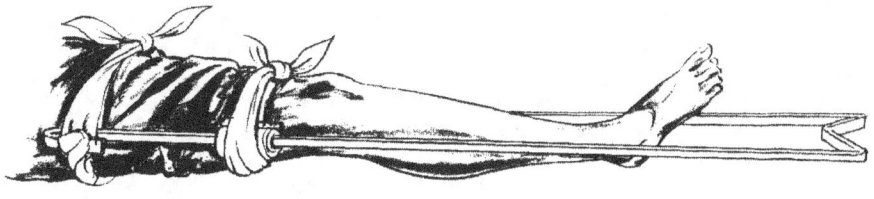

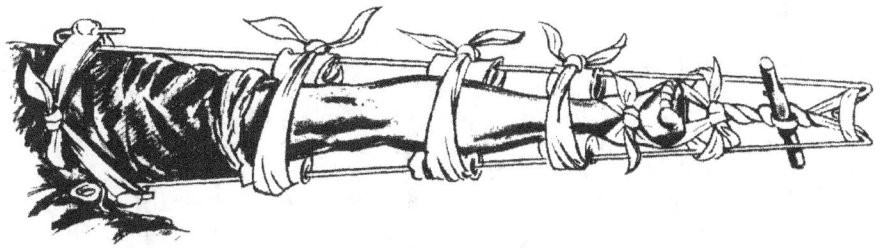

Before applying traction the necessary splinting material should be checked to be sure it is long enough and strong enough to maintain the desired amount of traction after the splint is applied. Do not attempt to use traction unless you have someone to assist you.

After a fracture occurs the muscles contract and may make traction difficult or impossible except under anesthesia. The length of time for this contraction to occur varies with the severity of the fracture.

Never Force Traction. If the muscles have not contracted, traction may be applied with a steady even "pull" or traction.

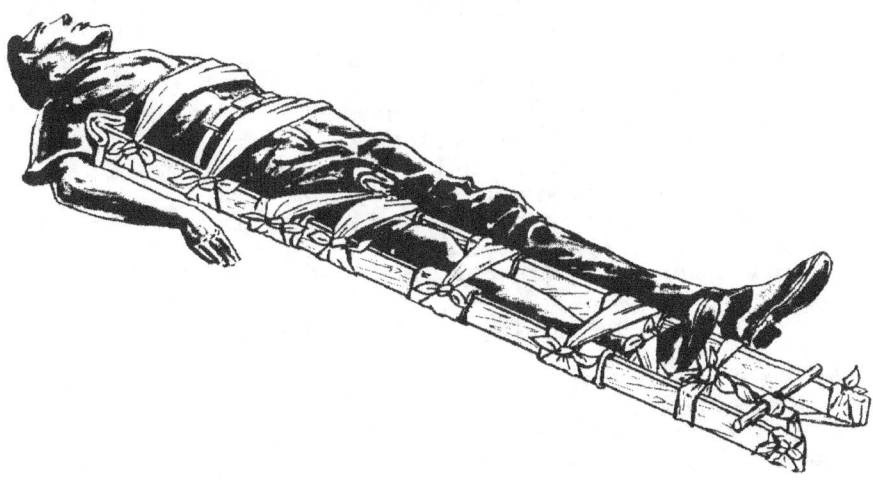

The half-circle of twisted cloth is securely fastened to the top of the splint and placed so that it fits around the outside of the upper leg and into the crease of the body between the buttocks and upper leg. The improvised splint in this picture is a curtain rod which has been bent to the desired shape, other improvised methods may be used. In the case of a fracture of the upper leg (femur) the outside splint should be extended alongside the body to just below the armpit and held in place at several points by ties extending completely around the chest and abdomen.

Caution: Be sure that the blood supply has not been shut off in any manner. This should be checked often as the injured limb may start to swell and cause the ties to become too tight.

SPRAINS

Sprains are injuries to the soft tissues surrounding the joints, usually occurring because of sudden movements beyond the normal range of a joint. Ligaments, muscle tendons, and blood vessels are stretched and occasionally torn. Ankles, fingers, wrists, and knees are most often affected.

A fracture of a bone may occur at the time of a sprain. Therefore, all severe sprains should be treated by splinting. First apply a bandage support, being careful not to make it so tight that it will interfere with the flow of blood (stop circulation). If possible, apply cold packs to the sprain during the first 30 minutes following injury. To retard swelling, all sprains should be elevated on pillows and the injured person kept quiet. Use of a sprained joint should not be allowed until such use can be carried out with little or no pain. Continue the bandage support of a sprained joint, such as the ankle, during the early period of walking or use.

TRANSPORTATION OF THE INJURED

What To Do

1. Before transporting any sick or injured person:
   Bleeding should be stopped.
   Breathing should be established.
   Fractures should be splintered.
   Shock should be treated.
   All other lifesaving methods completed.
2. Determine carefully the type and seriousness of the injuries and condition of the injured person.
3. Give complete emergency treatment *before moving* the injured.
4. Be gentle in moving the injured person; have enough help to assure safe moving.
5. Always carry a stretcher to an injured person, not the person to the stretcher.
6. Stretchers should be used for the more seriously injured persons and for transporting the injured over a long distance.

7. Be sure the person will not slip or fall from the stretcher while being carried. Belts or strong cloth bindings such as sheets may be used to secure the person to the stretcher.

8. Always use a two-man carry in preference to a one-man carry, if a hand carry is used. This helps to make the person being carried more comfortable, enables him to be carried farther, and is less likely to aggravate fractures or other serious injuries.

9. The various hand carries should not be used unless the person needs only slight support for short distances; or in case of emergencies where delay will endanger life. Examples—fire or explosion.

TRANSPORTING INJURED PERSONS

Do not be in a hurry to move an injured person.

First aid authorities report that more harm is probably done through improper transportation of injured persons than through any other measure of emergency assistance. The danger of causing paralysis or death in moving persons with head, back, or neck injuries has already been noted. Thus, before considering moving an injured person, except under the most urgent conditions, such as exposure to fire or fallout, you should make a careful check for all possible injuries so that you will know the right method of transporting him.

You should also make sure that bleeding is controlled, that the injured person is breathing satisfactorily, and that any possible broken bones have been splinted or, as in the case of neck or back fractures, are properly supported. Only then should you attempt to move him.

There are many ways of moving an injured person, depending upon the nature and location of injuries. Some of the most useful are illustrated. It is important to lift and carry a person gently, moving him slowly and carefully without jerky movements.

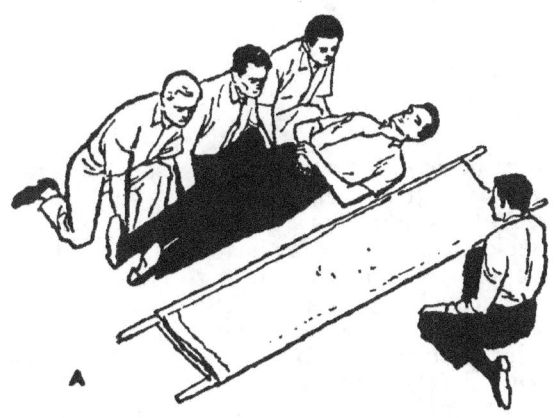

This is the first step in the correct method of using four people to load a seriously injured person on a stretcher. In this first step the fourth man does not touch the injured person.

The three persons now lift slowly and all together and roll the injured person gently toward them on injured side.

The fourth man now places the stretcher into position and then assists in lowering the person into the stretcher. Even, slow motion assures greatest safety and comfort of the injured person.

If it becomes absolutely necessary to move a person to safety *before* a thorough check of injuries can be made, you should try to *protect all parts of his body from the tension of lifting.* A body should never be jackknifed (lifted by head and heels only). Try to give adequate support to each extremity, to the head and the back, and to keep the entire body in a straight line.

If you are alone with an injured person who must be moved, and are unable to *carry* him, you may be able to *pull* him to safety. He should be pulled in the direction of the long axis of his body, not sideways. Danger of injuring him is less if a blanket (or similar object) can be placed under him, so that he can ride the blanket.

This saddle-back carry is simple and effective for moving an injured person a short distance, when his injuries are not serious.

A

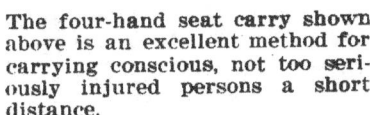

The four-hand seat carry shown above is an excellent method for carrying conscious, not too seriously injured persons a short distance.

B

C

This is an effective method of carrying an unconscious injured person a short distance provided it is not necessary to keep him flat.

BURNS

What To Do

Treat for shock.
Relieve pain.
Prevent infection.
Cover burned area with dry sterile or clean cloth.
Encourage fluids to replace fluid loss from body.
Give water, salt and soda solution: 1 teaspoonful salt and ½ teaspoonful soda to 1 quart water.

What Not To Do

DO NOT pull clothes over burned area.
DO NOT remove pieces of cloth that stick to burn.
DO NOT try to clean the burn.
DO NOT break blisters.
DO NOT use grease—ointment—petroleum jelly or any type of medication on severe burns.
DO NOT use iodine or antiseptics on burns.
DO NOT touch burn with anything except sterile or clean dressing.
DO NOT change dressings that were initially applied until absolutely necessary. They may be left in place 5-7 days.

The seriousness of a burn depends upon its extent (amount of body surface involved) and "degree" (depth of destruction of tissues). There are three recognized degrees:

1. In first degree burns, the skin is merely reddened as by a slight sunburn.

2. In second degree burns, blisters develop.

3. In third degree burns, there is deeper destruction, and the burned area may appear either charred or white.

It is difficult or impossible to determine the degree of a burn at first. It often appears less deep than it actually is. The degree may differ in different parts of the affected area.

First aid objectives are to treat for shock, relieve pain, and prevent infection. In all extensive burns, shock and infection are major hazards. The danger of infection is greatest in second- and third-degree burns.

A burn should be covered with a sterile dressing and a bandage to hold the dressing firmly in place. Pain is common to almost all burns and is caused partly by contact with the air. The even pressure of a bandage will help reduce pain.

The area around the burn should be carefully washed with soap and water for a distance of several inches, wiping away from the burn. The gauze dressing will prevent surface washings from entering the burned area.

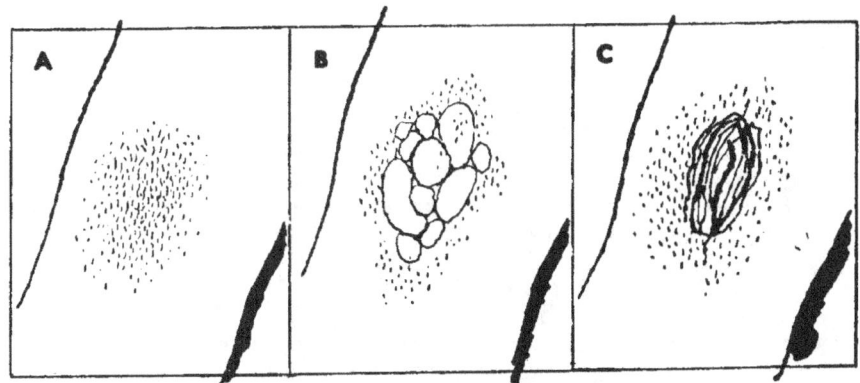

A first degree burn only reddens the skin and if it does not cover more than 25 per cent of the body, usually is not serious.

In second degree burns blisters develop and there is now the very real danger of infection. Extensive second degree burns will require giving additional fluids to the burned person. Do not apply grease or salve. Cover with sterile or clean dressing.

Third degree burns even in a relatively small area are serious. The injury is deep and the underlying tissue has been destroyed. Keep this type of burn clean to avoid infection.

If a sterile dressing is not available, or is not big enough to cover a large burned area, use a clean towel or sheet. The dressing should be thick enough to keep air out of the burned area. Do not touch a burn or breathe directly on it. Do not attempt to open blisters or remove bits of dirt or debris from the burned surface. The blisters are not harmful and they protect the underlying tissues against entry of germs until the dressing is applied.

If adjoining surfaces of skin are burned, be sure they are separated by gauze—for example, between toes and fingers, between ears and head, between folds of the groin and genital region, and in the armpits. Otherwise they may stick together. The dressing on a serious burn should be left on as long as possible.

No ointments or salves should be used on burns. Never use iodine or any other antiseptic on burns. Dressings should be dry.

A person with an extensive burn needs a lot of liquid and salt. Give him a half glass of a salt and baking soda solution every 15 minutes. You can make this solution by mixing a teaspoon of salt and a half teaspoon of baking soda in a quart of water. If you have salt and soda tablets, use as directed on the packages.

Continue to give liquid each 15 minutes for 2 or 3 hours. If the burn is large and severe, give the person as much liquid as he can comfortably take. In the first 24 hours, he could well take 1 quart for every 20 pounds of his body weight. *Do not force him to drink. His own thirst is the best guide.*

For chemical burns, where the skin has been irritated by chemicals, the chemical should be washed away with generous amounts of water. Treatment can then be carried out as previously described for other burns.

SHOCK

What To Do

1. Keep the person lying down.
2. Keep head lower than legs and hips if no chest or head injury.
3. Have head and shoulders slightly raised with chest or head injury or difficulty in breathing.
4. Keep the person from chilling.
5. Encourage fluids by mouth if person is conscious. Use solution of 1 teaspoonful salt and ½ teaspoonful baking soda to 1 quart of water. Give ½ glassful every 15 minutes.
6. Never attempt to give fluids to an unconscious person.
7. Alcohol should not be used as a stimulant.

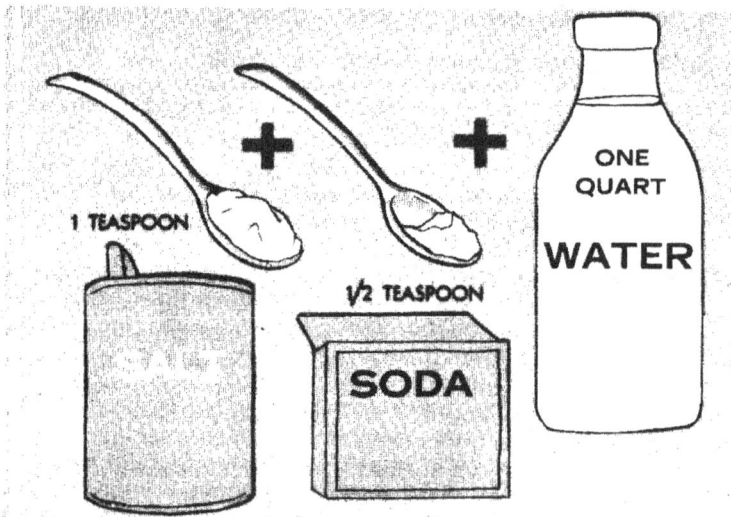

"Shock" as used in this section refers to a condition that frequently comes with serious injury such as severe wounds, burns, bleeding, and broken bones. It is due to a shortage of blood in various parts of the body. This causes the heart to beat faster in order to pump more blood, resulting in a rapid pulse. Lack of enough circulation through the brain causes unconsciousness.

Obviously a large amount of bleeding increases the danger of shock. In severe burns the oozing of blood fluids from the burned area increases the danger. *Shock may cause death if not treated promptly even though the injury which causes it may not itself be enough to cause death.*

Shock is easy to recognize. The skin gets pale and clammy, with small drops of sweat particularly around the lips and forehead. The person may complain of nausea and dizziness. His pulse may be fast and weak and his breathing shallow and irregular. His eyes may be dull with enlarged pupils, or he may be unconscious. A person may not be aware of the seriousness of his injury, then suddenly collapse.

All seriously injured persons should be treated for shock even though all of these symptoms have not appeared and the person seems normal and alert. Treatment for shock may prevent its development.

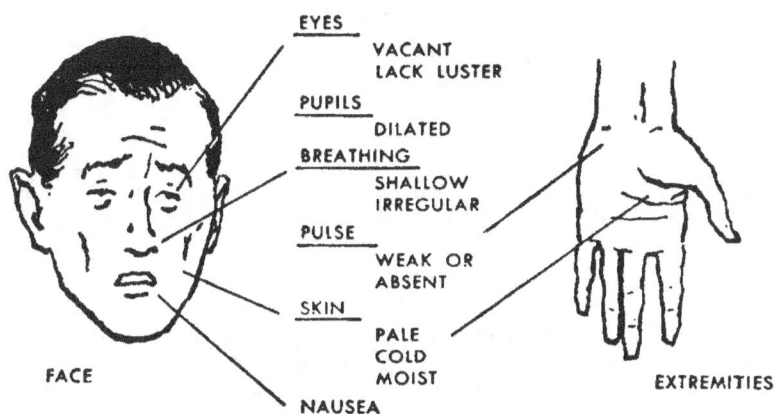

EYES
VACANT
LACK LUSTER

PUPILS
DILATED

BREATHING
SHALLOW
IRREGULAR

PULSE
WEAK OR
ABSENT

SKIN
PALE
COLD
MOIST

FACE

NAUSEA

EXTREMITIES

TREATMENT FOR SHOCK

1. Have the injured person lie down.
2. Elevate his feet and legs 12 inches or more. This helps the flow of blood to his heart and head. *Exception:* If the person has received a head or chest injury, or if he has difficulty breathing, elevate his head and chest rather than his feet.
3. Keep the person warm, but not hot. Place a blanket under him. Depending on the weather, place a sheet or blanket over him. Avoid getting him so hot that he perspires, for this draws blood to the skin, and away from the interior of his body where it is needed. On warm days or in a hot room no covering will be necessary.

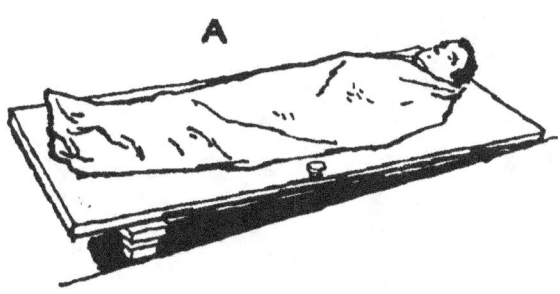

A

If a person does not have a head or chest injury and is in shock he should be placed in a headdown position. Keep the injured person warm.

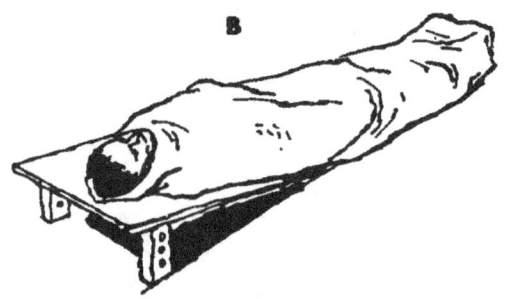

This is the correct position for a person in shock who has received either head or chest injuries. Raise the head only enough to prevent the blood from gathering in the upper part of the body. Keep the person warm.

4. Give him liquid, about a glassful of salt and soda solution every 15 minutes if his condition permits. If he is unconscious, do not attempt to give anything to drink. If he vomits or is nauseated, postpone giving liquid until the nausea disappears.

5. Keep the person quiet. See that bleeding is controlled and injured parts are kept still. Assure him that he will get the best care you can give. Reassurance is a potent medicine.

6. A person who has recovered from shock needs to be kept in bed. This is usually not difficult to accomplish as he will feel weak and exhausted. Sleep and rest will hasten his recovery.

SECTION III

Part 1 **NURSING CARE OF SICK AND INJURED (Alphabetically arranged by disease or medical problem)**

Part 2 **INFANT AND CHILD CARE**

NURSING CARE OF SICK AND INJURED

There may be ill members of the family to care for following a nuclear attack. Some cases will occur in the normal course of events and others will be brought on by the anxieties, difficulties, and crowding of shelter living. Fortunately, the human body has a remarkable ability to overcome disease and withstand stress. If you are prepared to assist with intelligent and encouraging care, there is much you can do to help the sick even though a doctor is not available.

See your doctor now and talk over with him how you should treat special illnesses which might occur in your family. If there are children, a pregnant woman, elderly persons, or a chronically ill member of the family, your doctor can tell you the emergencies that could come up and how to handle them. This applies especially to heart disease, diabetes, asthma, stomach ulcers, and other illnesses of a long-term nature.

It will be helpful to keep a written record of the symptoms, treatment, reactions, temperature, and changes in condition of sick or injured persons in your family in order to have this information for a doctor when one becomes available. After the first emergency period following enemy attack, communications may be restored and you may be able to get advice by telephone from a physician even though he cannot make a personal visit.

Some of the things suggested under "General Procedures," and also in some of the more specific sections which follow, will need to be modified to fit the particular situation you face. For example, some methods of care, routine under normal conditions, will be impossible in a fallout shelter, and some things possible in one shelter may not be in others because of differences in supplies or availability of utilities. (If you have cooking facilities and water, you can boil the water; if your electric refrigerator still works, you may have ice available for an ice bag, etc.)

Some kinds of care that will be possible for you to give will not be as *necessary* to give as others. You will have to decide the most important uses of your limited supplies.

Perhaps nowhere will this be truer than in your use of water. For example, in "General Procedures," the method of giving water sponge baths is described. Such baths are *helpful* in making any sick person feel more comfortable, but they are *important* in reducing fever. Thus, if you have sufficient water, you can give sponge baths to anyone who might be refreshed by them, but where water is in short supply, you will have to save it for the most urgent health uses. In such a situation you should restrict sponge baths to persons in real need of them.

GENERAL PROCEDURES

All sick people benefit from knowing that someone is interested in helping them and in giving them the best care possible. Tell a sick person that you will care for him and it will help him get well. Make him as comfortable as possible, and be cheerful and reassuring.

Some people will benefit most from complete bed rest; others by being given small jobs to do to keep their minds off their own distress.

A refreshed body and mouth make a sick person feel better. To give a sponge bath, wash and dry one part of the body at a time, keeping the other parts covered. Start with the head and face, then the chest and abdomen, arms and back, and end with the legs and feet.

If the patient can sit up, hold a basin in his lap and let him brush his teeth. If he cannot sit up, prepare his toothbrush and turn his head to one side. Hold a basin under his chin. Then let him brush his teeth on one side. Turn his head and have him brush the other side.

Feeding a helpless person requires patience and skill. First, see that he is comfortable. Then sit down beside him and feed him slowly from the side of the spoon. Be sure that the food or liquid is not too hot. Touch his lower lip with the side of the spoon and then tip the spoon into his mouth. Allow him time to swallow after each spoonful.

When helping him to drink from a cup, support his head with your hand under his pillow. Let him guide the cup and control the rate of flow with his hand under the cup, while you continue to hold the handle.

Do not be alarmed if a sick person has no appetite. Do not force him to eat. If constipation is a problem, enemas, suppositories, or laxatives may be given for relief, the choice depending upon individual preference, the age of the patient, and availability of materials.

A person who stays in bed for a period of time may get bedsores because of continued pressure on parts of the body, particularly the base of the spine, elbows, heels, shoulders, and hips. To prevent or relieve this situation, change the person's position frequently from one side to another and from back to stomach. Tender areas may be raised off the bed. For example, a stocking stuffed with cotton can be shaped like a large doughnut for the elbow or heel to rest in.

You can improvise some necessary items for bed care. A basin or a cardboard carton lined with folded newspapers may be used as a bedpan. A glass jar or tin can with rounded edges may be used as a urinal. A receptacle for soiled dressings and human wastes can be made from folded newspapers.

Pain in any part of the body may be reduced by giving one or two ordinary 5-grain aspirin tablets to an adult every 4 hours for as long as the pain continues. The dosage for children under 5 years of age is one grain per year of age. Thus, for young children, it will be necessary to divide the adult size 5-grain tablet, or to use children's aspirin which comes in 1¼-grain tablets. Children from 5 to 10 years of age can take one 5-grain tablet; over 10 consider as an adult.

Any chronically ill person who regularly takes medicine, such as digitalis or insulin, should always keep at least a 2-month supply on hand. (Insulin may be stored at room temperature for a period of weeks without losing its potency.) Asthmatics and persons suffering from peptic ulcer should be sure they have sufficient amounts of their special medicines.

Elderly persons should not be allowed to remain lying down most of the time but should be encouraged to be up and around to the fullest extent their condition will permit. They should be given jobs that they can do easily. They should not be permitted to go without food for very long.

Older persons who have difficulty passing their urine, as in prostatic disease, should discuss with their doctor the advisability of including a catheter in their emergency medical supplies. If they plan to do so, they should be instructed regarding its use.

ABSCESSES AND BOILS

What To Do

1. Leave it alone if it is closed.
2. Wait for it to open by itself.
3. Cover with a sterile or clean dressing if it is draining.
4. Apply hot packs if possible.
5. Give aspirin for pain.
6. When possible keep clothing away from area to prevent spreading infection.

What Not To Do

DO NOT squeeze a pimple, boil, or carbuncle.
DO NOT prick it with a pin or needle.
DO NOT lance it or open it.

An abscess is a raised area, full of pus when ripe, usually the result of an infection. It may occur anywhere on the body. Germs may enter the body through a wound or break in the skin, or one of the natural body openings. The abcess is caused by the body's defenses against the spread of infection. A mass is formed and the area of infection is walled off. The abscess may be located deep in the body so that there is no outward sign. There may be fever and a general feeling of illness. If the abscess is near the surface, there will probably be swelling, tenderness, and pain, and the skin will feel hot to the touch. If the abscess is draining, great care must be taken to destroy the dressings which have been used so that the drainage from the abscess will not touch and contaminate anything. The person giving the care must wash his hands thoroughly after handling dressings or other materials used.

Boils, pimples, and carbuncles are infections of the skin. Any area of the skin which is frequently rubbed or irritated is a good site for germs from the outside to collect. The back of the neck, the armpits and the area around the buttocks are frequent sites of boils. They may occur on the face, arms, legs, and ears. Boils around the nose, lips, and eyes are dangerous because the blood vessels from those areas drain toward the brain and might carry infection to it.

Cleanliness of person and clothing is the best prevention of boils. In a situation where keeping clean is difficult, boils may occur frequently. The body tries to wall off the infection and a round, reddened, painful, peaklike elevation develops on the surface of the skin. A core may form in the center. A pimple is a small version of a boil and a carbuncle is a deeper, more extensive and more painful type. A carbuncle may be accompanied by chills and fever and the person may feel generally ill. Do not squeeze a pimple, boil, or carbuncle. Do not prick it with a pin. This would break down the protective wall around the infection and allow its spread. If it is small, leave it alone. Use a sterile dressing, or the cleanest material available, to cover the boil if it is draining.

ANIMAL BITES

What To Do

1. Wash the wound thoroughly with soap and water.
2. Catch the animal and confine for 14 days (if practical).

Animal bites (those made by dogs and cats are most common) always involve the danger of infection since there are many germs on an animal's teeth and in its mouth, but in addition such bites may carry the greater risk of rabies, sometimes called hydrophobia. The virus or germ of this disease is present in the saliva of rabid animals. Rabies can attack humans as well as animals. Rabies is usually a fatal disease once it has developed; however, the incubation period is such that if the animal can be confined and watched for a period of 14 days and it is determined that the animal was rabid, the Pasteur treatment may be given to the person who has been bitten. This treatment consists of a series of injections usually given once a day for 14 days. The incubation period is rarely less than 15 days, therefore, if it is suspected that the person may have been bitten by a rabid animal, this person should be given early consideration for movement from the shelter to commence the Pasteur treatment after being seen by a physician.

It is unlikely that adequate laboratory facilities will be available to determine whether or not the animal was rabid; however, if the animal has been confined and has not died in 14 days the chances are excellent that it was not rabid. If it is rabid, it will, after several days, show what are called "furious" symptoms. Shortly thereafter the animal becomes paralyzed and dies.

Scratches caused by animals with other than their teeth should be washed thoroughly with soap and water and then treated as any other injury. If infection should follow refer to "Infection" section of this manual.

ASTHMA ATTACK

What To Do

1. Place victim in comfortable sitting position.
2. Reassure the victim.
3. Determine if he has his own medication.
4. Administer his medication ONLY AFTER checking with victim as to EXACT DOSAGE AND PROPER ADMINIS-TRATION.

When a person is suffering an asthma attack his breathing is usually labored, difficult and accompanied by wheezing or squeaking sounds. Frequent coughing is likely. The victim of an asthmatic attack looks anxious and stressed as he struggles to get air IN and OUT of his lungs.

This breathing difficulty results from changes in the air passages so that air cannot pass freely to and from the tiny air sacks in the lungs. Such changes may be caused by an allergy or sensitivity to some foreign substance such as dust or pollen. In which case, the attack is known as bronchial asthma. Asthma may also result from a heart condition. This type is called cardiac asthma.

A person suffering an asthma attack usually has a dusky or bluish color of the lips if the attack is severe. In the recurrent or chronic type of asthma, the person may be pale around the mouth and eyes and in a cold sweat. The temperature is usually normal unless there is an accompanying infection.

A person suffering an asthma attack can usually breathe more easily if he is in a sitting position or leaning slightly forward with hands braced on knees. He should be made as comfortable as possible and supported where possible in the position that gives him the greatest ease of breathing. Try to reassure the victim and allay his fears. Keep him quiet and where possible place him near the air intake to the shelter.

BLISTERS

What To Do

1. Wash blister area clean.
2. Sterilize a needle.
3. Open blister from edge.
4. Gently squeeze out fluid and cover with dressing.
5. Keep it clean.

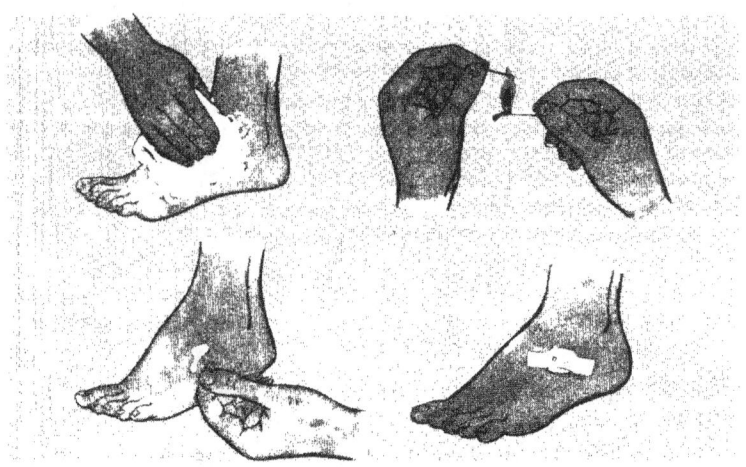

Blisters not caused by burns may result on the skin when it has been subjected to repeated pressures and excessive rubbing. They are not uncommon on the feet from poorly fitting stockings or shoes, or on the hands from using unfamiliar equipment or doing unaccustomed work. They should be cared for to prevent serious infection from developing.

Do not attempt to remove the dead skin which formed the blister. Let it stay on as long as possible to provide protection to the tender underlying tissue and assist in the prevention of infection.

CHILLS

What To Do

1. Put person to bed.
2. Keep person warm.

A chill or sudden cold feeling will usually be associated with fever. A chill is usually a sign of some disorder, perhaps only of a minor nature. A person should rest and keep warm. Severe chills accompanied with shivering are usually a sign of a more serious ailment providing the temperature of the shelter is obviously not the prime cause. The person will usually have a chill and shiver for a short period and then will suddenly feel very hot and flushed. The person should be placed in bed and kept as warm as possible. Additional clothing and blankets will usually *not* stop the chill and shivering, but will make the person a little more comfortable.

Caution: During the period of intermittent chills and fever the person should be watched carefully to prevent him throwing off all the covering during the period of the fever and then not being covered again when the chills occur. Even though these signs and symptoms may indicate a severe illness do not attempt to diagnose the illness. *Only treat the symptom, never try to diagnose. Make the patient comfortable as possible. Give aspirin for relief of aches and pains.*

46

CHOKING

What To Do

Hold as shown above—a vigorous slap on the back will help dislodge obstruction in throat.

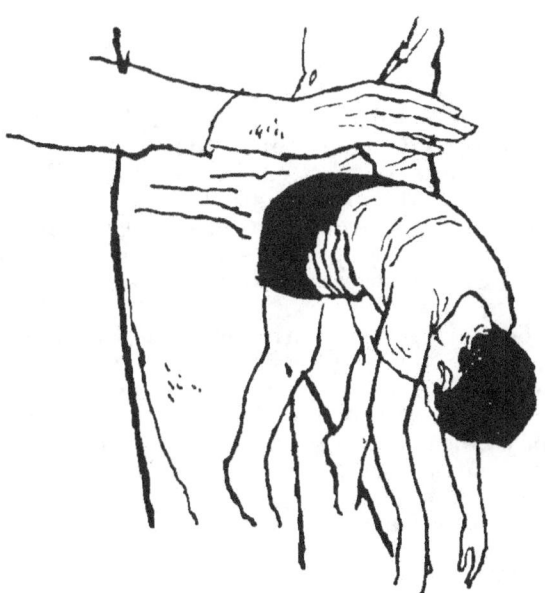

When objects are caught in the throats of children and cannot be reached with the fingers, they may be dislodged as shown above. If breathing stops quickly try above methods of removing obstruction and start artificial respiration immediately.

When a person's windpipe becomes blocked, he chokes and becomes red in the face. If the windpipe is not cleared, he will suffocate.

Usually, a sharp blow on the back between the shoulder blades will remove the material blocking the air passage into the lungs. If not, bend him over and strike again. A small child should be held upside down and hit between the shoulder blades.

COMMON COLD

What To Do

1. For adults two aspirins every 4 hours. For children one aspirin every 4 hours.
2. Drink ample amounts of fluids, preferably fruit juices if available.
3. Get as much rest as possible.
4. Use nose drops from medical kit.

Prevent Others From Catching Your Cold

1. Cover your mouth with a paper tissue or handkerchief when coughing, or sneezing.
2. Dispose of tissues or handkerchiefs promptly after they have been used.
3. Wash your hands thoroughly before preparing or handling food for others.

In the crowded conditions of a shelter, it will probably be impossible to keep colds from spreading since there is no way to isolate sick persons. In most cases, the colds will be over in 4 or 5 days. Aspirin and cough mixture, as well as usual household remedies to which you are accustomed, may help relieve some of the discomfort. The sick person should cover his mouth and nose when coughing and sneezing, and dispose carefully of tissues used to wipe his nose.

If symptoms are severe, with fever and aches, the sick person should stay in bed and drink as much liquid as can be spared. It would be best if only one person took care of him while the others remain as far away as possible.

A cold may be the first sign of a more serious illness, especially in children. Measles, mumps, whooping cough, and other diseases often begin with signs of a cold. A child with cold symptoms should be isolated as much as possible.

SORE THROAT

Sore throat occurs very commonly. It may be a local inflammation affecting only the throat, or it may seriously affect the entire body, as in diphtheria or streptococcal sore throat.

Sore throat often begins with general symptoms of listlessness, headache, muscle pains, a slight chill or chilly feeling, and fever. The throat feels sore, particularly on swallowing. Within a few hours, the tonsils and throat may be swollen and red; the tongue coated. If inflammation progresses sufficiently, swallowing will be difficult.

For sore throat, a gargle of hot water and salt (one teaspoon to a pint), or aspirin solution (4 tablets to a pint) every 3 hours, may be all that is needed. Smoking should be discouraged. Cold compresses, if available, placed over the throat may be comforting. Aspirin may be given every 4 hours as needed and laxatives if constipation is present. Liquids should be given freely and a liquid or soft diet is best.

CONVULSIONS

What To Do

1. Keep the person from hurting himself.
2. If you can without using force, slip something like a folded handkerchief or a piece of rubber (nothing hard) between his teeth to keep him from biting his tongue or cheek. Do not force the jaw open.

What Not To Do

DO NOT attempt to restrain the person having the attack, except to prevent him injuring himself.

No matter what the cause of the convulsion, little can be done to shorten the attack. *The most important thing is to prevent the person hurting himself.*

If he has fallen to the floor, move objects that he might strike. Put a pillow or some rolled clothing under his head. If his teeth are clenched don't try to pry them loose. However, if you can without using force, slip something like a folded handkerchief or a piece of rubber (nothing hard) between his teeth to keep him from biting his tongue or cheek. A blanket wrapped loosely around his legs will tend to control their thrashing about. If due to epilepsy, the convulsion will soon end. When it does, the person will be sleepy and should be allowed to sleep as long as he wishes. He may be very irritable and have no memory of the convulsion.

In a child or infant, convulsions may occur with high fever. Efforts should be made to reduce the fever. Give aspirin, if the patient is able to swallow. Sponge his body with lukewarm water.

CROUP

Croup usually begins suddenly at night when the child wakens with a hoarse cough, and has difficulty in breathing. Croup may accompany a cold, but it sometimes develops when there is no other evidence of a cold.

Inhalation of steam from boiling water provides the best means of relief. A kettle or vaporizer filled with water and kept boiling at a safe distance from the bed will provide warm moist air in the room and will be of benefit in cases of croup, asthma, bronchitis, and laryngitis.

If the attack is severe and humidity in the room as described above is not sufficient, you may improvise a croup tent to bring the steam more directly to the patient. Drape a towel or sheet over the head of the patient's bed and direct the steam from the kettle spout through a long paper tube or funnel into the tent. The steam should be directed toward the top of the improvised tent and away from the patient's face. Stay close at hand to see that the patient is not burned by either the kettle or the steam. If it is not possible to provide steam, warm compresses applied to the chest and throat may give some relief.

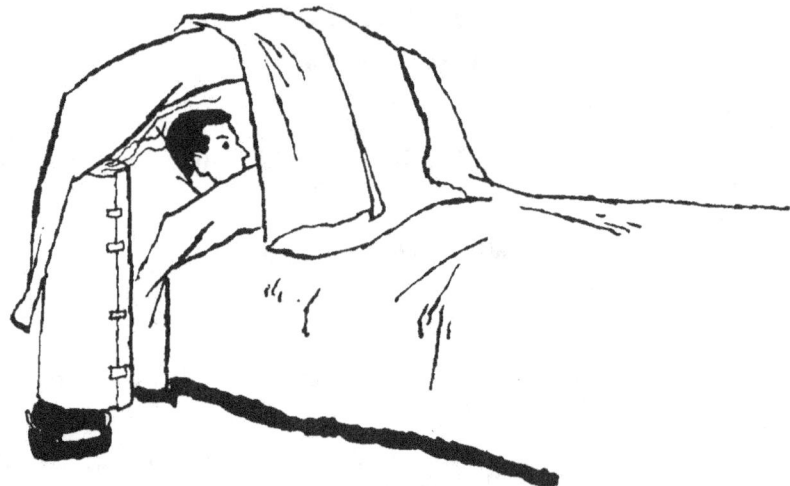

Steam inhalations may be given to those suffering from croup, bronchitis, laryngitis, asthma, colds, or other respiratory conditions. It adds humidity to air. Make tent over a frame and direct paper cone to top of tent, away from person's face. Always direct steam away from person's face. It will burn any exposed area.

DIABETIC EMERGENCIES

What To Do

1. Put the victim to bed.
2. Prop him in a partial sitting up position.
3. Keep him warm.
4. Read carefully the first two paragraphs on the next page and take the appropriate action.

Remember—There are two types of diabetic emergencies. One which results from LACK OF INSULIN, and one which results from TOO MUCH INSULIN.

Diabetic persons may become unconscious if they fail to take enough insulin or if they take too much.

If there is a *lack of insulin*, the person's face becomes flushed, his lips bright red, and he becomes sleepy and perhaps unconscious. This condition is known as diabetic coma. He breathes in gasps and his breath has an odor like nail polish remover. If insulin is available, give him his regular dose. If it is not available, make him as comfortable as possible.

To prevent diabetic coma, diabetics must make sure they have a sufficient supply of insulin on hand. As previously recommended, a diabetic person should maintain a 2-month emergency supply of insulin. If he sees his supply dwindling and fears that it will not be sufficient to maintain him until further insulin can be obtained, he should reduce his regular insulin dosage and also his need for it by cutting his food intake, particularly of carbohydrates.

A person who suffers from *too much insulin* will have an ashy white face with moist clammy skin. He will usually perspire a great deal and he may become unconscious. Such a person desperately needs sugar. If he is still conscious, give him a teaspoonful of sugar, a piece of chocolate, sips of a sugar and water solution, or orange juice, if available. If unconscious, place a teaspoonful of moistened sugar under his tongue. It will be absorbed into his blood. Recovery will usually be rapid.

DIARRHEA

What To Do

1. Withhold any food for 24 hours.
2. Give water if person does not also have nausea and vomiting.
3. If diarrhea persists for 2 to 3 days give person sugar-salt solution. (Dissolve 1 level teaspoonful of salt and 1½ tablespoonfuls of sugar in a quart of water.)
4. If diarrhea mixture is available in medical kit give as directed on label.
5. When diarrhea stops give warm liquid or soft diet.
6. Be extremely careful in handling the stools of person to prevent infection of yourself or others.

From earliest times, the condition most commonly associated with insanitary living has been diarrhea. Sources of infection are polluted water, milk, or other foods, and the discharges of patients or carriers of the disease. The germs which cause diarrhea are usually spread by contaminated hands and by flies. There may be considerable diarrhea in the crowded conditions of shelter living, but this illness can be prevented. The number of bowel movements may vary from 5 to 25 in a day, depending upon the severity of the case, but the amount of material excreted from the bowels each time is usually very small and consists largely of water, sometimes mucus, and occasionally blood.

Replacement of fluids lost by frequent bowel movements is important. All patients should have bed rest and be kept warm. Use your diarrhea medication as previously directed by your doctor. Other measures to be taken can be more easily considered by age groups:

Infants—If a baby under 1 year of age is having diarrhea, it is desirable to omit one or two feedings or give smaller amounts of feeding. Reduced feedings may be given as follows:

If the baby is breast-fed, let him nurse for only half as long as usual and, after the feeding, give him as much boiled water as he will take. If the baby is bottle-fed dilute the milk mixture with an equal amount of boiled water and let him take as much as he wants. As the baby gets better and is ready for more food, it may be given to him until finally he is taking all of his regular feeding—milk and whatever other foods he took before he became sick.

Children, 1–10—After the onset of diarrhea, discontinue all food for 24 hours. The child should be given water to drink. If the diarrhea is severe, instead of plain water substitute the following sugar-salt water solution: into 1 quart of water dissolve 1 level teaspoon of table salt and 1½ tablespoonful of sugar.

After 24 hours, a liquid diet of broth or beef stock soups may be given, and as the patient improves a light diet of low residue foods may be started. These include such things as refined wheat cereals, soda crackers, macaroni, rice, potatoes, and jello. Avoid such foods as whole grain products, raw fruits and vegetables, fried meats, cream soups, and spices. Milk intake should be restricted to one pint a day.

Adults—Discontinue food for 24 hours. Replace fluids by giving water, sugar and saltwater solution, black coffee, or tea, as tolerated. After 24 hours, a diet following the pattern described above for children may be started.

EARACHE

What To Do

1. Apply ice bag or hot water bottle to affected ear. (Try the ice bag first and if this doesn't bring relief, switch to the hot water bottle.)
2. Apply two or three drops of ear drops from the medical kit.
3. Give aspirin for pain.

What Not To Do

DO NOT use any kind of ear drops in ear that is discharging fluid.

Ear drops may give relief in the case of severe earache.

Do not use any kind of ear drops in an ear that is discharging pus, unless so instructed by your physician.

If possible, ear drops should be warmed before use. Heat the bottle of drops by immersing it in warm water. Do not get it too hot. Test the temperature of the drops on your wrist before using.

Have the patient lie down with his head turned to the side, the aching ear up. Hold the tip of the medicine dropper at the opening of the ear canal and drop in from 2 to 4 of the warmed drops. Do not insert the dropper into the canal. You can help straighten the ear canal so that the drops can slide down into it by grasping the upper part of the ear and pulling it gently toward the back and top of the head. Ask the patient to keep his head turned to the side for a few minutes to allow the drops to move down into the ear.

Aspirin may help reduce the pain. The application of warmth to the outside of the ear with a hot-water bottle, cloth dipped in warm water, or electric heating pad (if power is available) may give some additional relief.

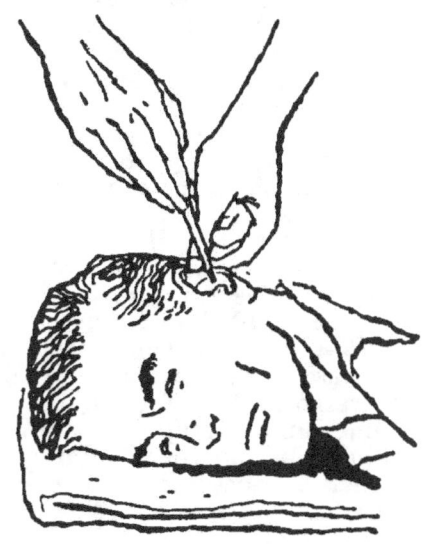

Persons with earache should be lying down on unaffected side so that ear is readily accessible. Grasp the ear and pull back and up. This straightens the ear canal. Put 2–4 drops of warm oil in ear. Do not touch ear with medicine dropper. Do not put drops in an ear which is discharging pus.

EMOTIONAL PROBLEMS

SYMPTOMS: Apathy, blank expression, crying, nervous laughter, moodiness, irritability, untidiness, avoiding crowds, or overconfidence.

What To Do

1. First of all—STAY CALM!
2. Be confident in your ability to handle the situation.
3. Use authority. Authority creates a feeling of security in the people.
4. Give the person hot coffee, warm soup, or food.

5. If bordering on hysterics, give maximum of four aspirin tablets and try to get him to lie down and sleep.

6. Assign specific duties when person is able to do them.

7. Keep the person busy.

8. Encourage recreational activities.

What Not To Do

1. DO NOT scold or talk harshly.

2. DO NOT give alcohol or narcotics.

3. DO NOT slap or strike.

Emotional problems may increase in a time of disaster, particularly under conditions of confined living. They will vary with the mental and physical condition of individuals.

Some persons will remain remarkably calm in an emergency. They will accept the situation as it is and do everything possible to be helpful.

Others may temporarily show signs of weakness, trembling, nausea, vomiting, uncontrollable crying, and excessive sweating. Their thinking will be confused and they will be jittery. But in most cases these symptoms will disappear in a short time as the person gets used to the situation.

Another type of person will sit or stand alone and act unaware of what has happened. He will not speak or reply to questions. He will show no concern for his safety and may need to be protected.

Some people will react in an opposite manner. They will talk rapidly, joke, and show too much confidence in meeting the situation. They may not accept suggestions from others and may prevent desirable action.

Persons with panic reactions are the most difficult to control because it is so hard to get their attention, yet it may be necessary to restrain them for their own safety and that of others. Their blind, unreasoning efforts to escape from the situation can affect others around them. Panic, if uncontrolled, is contagious. If gentle firmness doesn't work with them, physical force may be necessary to isolate them as far as possible from other members of the group.

Some people in an emergency will show their great anxiety by insisting that a part of their body no longer functions. For example, a leg or arm may appear to be paralyzed though no injury is apparent.

Such symptoms are the body's attempt to relieve extreme anxiety. This reaction is beyond the control of the person involved. He is actually just as disabled as one who is physically paralyzed even though his injury is emotional rather than physical.

A person's emotional reaction may change rapidly. Intense activity may be followed by numbness and a "don't care" attitude. At other times, he may appear to be perfectly normal.

Do not blame or make fun of anyone for feeling the way he does. If a man has a broken leg, no one expects him to walk. Similarly if a man's ability to cope with his personal situation is lost, no one should expect him to resume normal behavior at once. Telling him to "snap out of it" will not help. He does not want to feel the way he does. Try to understand his feelings, not tell him how he should feel. Give him sympathy and encouragement but not obvious pity.

Let the disturbed person talk freely of his feelings. Even a few minutes of talk will relieve him remarkably. Try to suggest a job or two he can do to help despite his problem. By showing an interest in him and bypassing his temporary difficulty, you will help him back to normal. A cup of warm soup or tea is a physical help you might offer.

EYE IRRITATIONS

What To Do

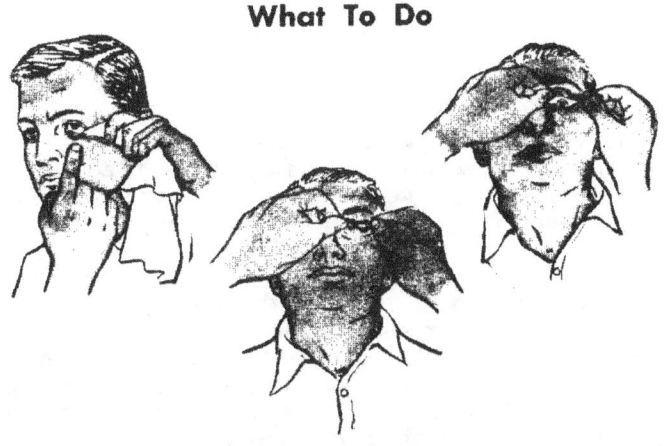

The eye must be treated very gently. Use the corner of a clean handkerchief to remove foreign object. If you do not see it on lower lid or eyeball, grasp upper lid and lashes, pull them down, place match or small twig over lid, and pull lid up and back over match. This will give you a good view of upper lid.

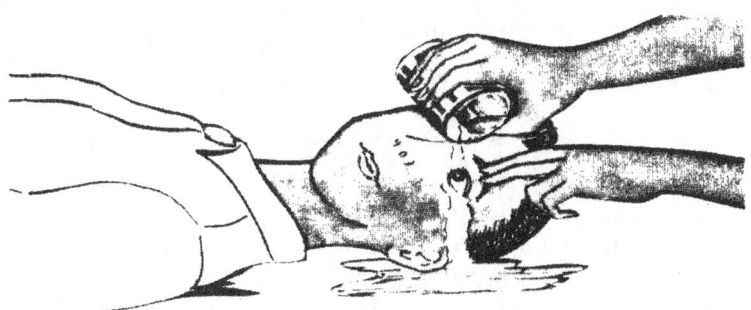

Remove chemicals and very fine dust by flushing with water. Turn head to one side. Use plenty of water. Hold glass or container close to nose.

Never rub the eye that has a foreign body (sand, cinder, insect) in it, since this may injure the delicate covering of the eyeball or imbed the object so that it will be more difficult to remove. Have the person close his eye so that tears will accumulate and perhaps wash out the object naturally. If the object can be seen, it often can be removed by touching it lightly with a sterile cotton-tipped applicator or the moistened corner of a clean handkerchief.

A weak salt solution, one teaspoonful of salt to a quart of water, may be used as an eye wash, and cold compresses to the eye will give some relief.

In a serious eye injury, it is advisable to cover both eyes with a sterile gauze dressing. It is important to rest the injured eye and this is best accomplished by covering both eyes.

FEVER

What To Do

1. Determine the amount of fever.
2. Put person to bed.
3. Give two aspirins every 4 hours.
4. When fever is severe (more than 102° in adults, and more than 103° in children) give sponge bath or apply cool compresses.
5. When fever and chills occur alternately, refer to section on chills.

Fever is a symptom of many kinds of disease, especially those caused by germs and viruses, in which the body temperature is elevated above normal limits. Normal temperature is usually considered to be 98.6° F. taken by mouth, or a degree higher, (99.6° F.) taken in the rectum. Actually, however, the "normal" temperature of healthy persons may fluctuate slightly above or below these figures without any evidence of disease. Temperatures in a patient suffering from an infection may often rise to 102 or 103 degrees and occasionally higher. A child's temperature usually rises more rapidly than an adult's, but also subsides quickly.

A person with fever looks flushed and feels hot to the touch. He may also complain of headaches or aches in his back, arms, or legs. He should stay in bed and should be encouraged to drink fluids. Food should be simple and light, depending on what he wants.

Aspirin will reduce fever and help relieve aches and pains. Two ordinary 5-grain tablets may be given to an adult every 4 hours as long as the fever lasts. The dosage for children would be the same as indicated under "General Procedures."

In children, whenever the temperature goes above 103 degrees by mouth or 104 by rectum, efforts should be made to reduce it. Give aspirin as indicated above. Sponging the body with cool water or rubbing alcohol, if available, will help reduce fever and make the patient feel much better. These same measures can be applied to adults with prolonged high fever. (See sponge bath directions under "General Procedures." If water is scarce, do not discard the sponging water after use. Retain and reuse it.

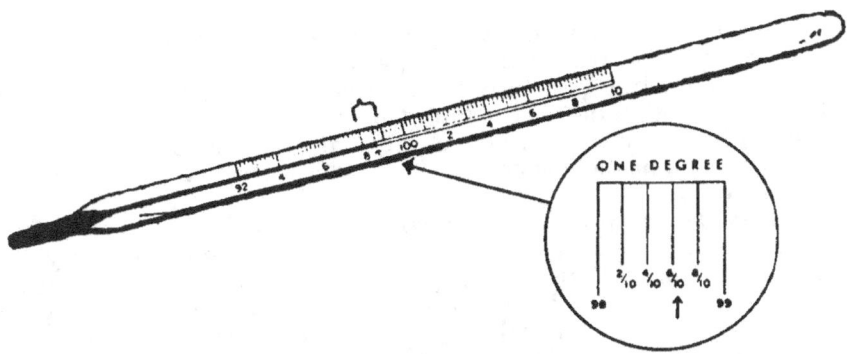

ONE DEGREE

A clinical thermometer is a useful household item. 98.6° F. is considered average normal. Learn to read thermometer by practicing. Hold in good light by tip and turn slowly toward you until you see the height of the silver mercury. Hold it level with your eyes. Handle it gently. Never put in hot water. Keep in case when not in use.

FROSTBITE

What To Do

1. Rapidly thaw frostbitten part of body.
    (a) Place affected part next to warm part of your body or warm part of somebody else's body, or
    (b) Place frostbitten part of body in lukewarm water (about 108°F), or
    (c) Cover affected area with scarves, clothing, blankets, etc.
2. Give hot coffee or hot tea.
3. Handle affected part with great care and gentleness.

What Not To Do

DO NOT rub the affected part.
DO NOT use *hot water.*
DO NOT use hot water bottle or heat lamps.
DO NOT disturb blisters if they develop.
DO NOT *rub with ice or snow.*

Exposure to dry cold causes the local injury known as frostbite. Parts of the body most likely to be frostbitten are the cheeks, nose, chin, ears, forehead, wrists, hands, and feet. Most cases of frostbite are caused by exposure to air below freezing temperatures.

The symptoms of frostbite vary depending on the severity of the injury. The frostbitten part is usually not painful, but is numb and stiff. The skin is first white or grayish white in color and then it becomes bright pink. If the exposure to cold continues the skin becomes white again.

When the frostbitten area is warmed it immediately becomes red and swollen and large blisters may develop. Severe frostbite causes the condition known as gangrene in which soft body tissue and sometimes even bone are permanently destroyed. In the course of healing, a gangrenous tissue is slipped off and leaves healthy tissue underneath, but if deep tissue has been destroyed, the injured part may require amputation. Persons with severe frostbite should be considered for priority movement when radiation level permits.

Early detection of frostbite will permit early treatment. Persons in a shelter which is improperly heated should not only frequently examine their own exposed parts but also those of other occupants for signs of frostbite. A grayish or white waxy appearance of the skin is an early sign of freezing. Whenever any part shows this sign start first aid at once. Distinct pain is usually not present as a warning that frostbite or freezing is occurring. Loss of feeling when the skin is touched is another important sign. In extremely cold weather stiffness caused by freezing can be detected by wrinkling of the face. *Contrary to popular belief rapid thawing of tissues frozen from relatively short exposures result in less loss of tissue than does slow thawing. Do not rub it with ice or snow.*

The correct treatment is directed toward the rapid thawing of the frozen tissue. To thaw a frostbitten part put it next to a warm part of your body or next to the warm part of someone else's body. For example, put your left hand under the right armpit. Extra cover with scarves, blankets, clothing, etc. will help in the rapid thawing process. Exposed parts, if possible, may also be placed in lukewarm water at about 108° F.

Caution: Rapid thawing with warmth is the correct care of this type of injury; however, *do not use hot water, hot water bottles or heat lamps. Do not place victim close to hot stove or furnace.* Extreme heats of the above type will cause greater tissue damage.

An arm or leg which has been frostbitten and then thawed should be placed in an elevated position and kept at rest.

HEADACHE

What To Do

1. Give two aspirins every 4 hours for adults; one aspirin every 4 hours for children.
2. Rest for a few hours.
3. If headache persists, put the person to bed.
4. Apply cold compresses to the forehead and back of neck.

There are many different causes for headaches and only a physician is capable of adequately determining their cause. Most minor headaches regardless of their cause will usually be promptly relieved by taking two aspirins every 4 hours for adults, and one aspirin every 4 hours for children. It is also important that immediately after taking the aspirin the person should either lie down or sit down and rest for a few hours. If the headache persists the person should go to bed to get complete rest. Cold compresses may be applied to the forehead and back of the neck. The average headache will soon be relieved with these procedures.

Those persons who are subject to migraine headaches usually carry with them the medication which has been prescribed by their physician. If the person does not have the proper medication with him but knows that they are experiencing a migraine headache, he may be given three aspirins every 4 hours followed by one or two cups of strong black coffee. Most persons with migraine headaches will be more comfortable partially sitting up in bed with their eyes covered to keep out the light.

Headaches will be very common among the occupants of a shelter as they are quite often brought about through worry and tension. Caution should be exercised not to use aspirin indiscriminately, nor to waste it on the milder type of headaches as later on during the shelter occupancy the aspirin may be needed for more acute situations.

To the best of his ability, the shelter manager should, through whatever communication is available, keep the shelter occupants constantly informed of activities outside the shelter and should keep the occupants occupied doing things for themselves and others in the shelter as much as possible. These actions alone will do much to reduce the problem of headaches.

HEART EMERGENCIES

What To Do

1. Administer medication.
2. Place person in a comfortable position, usually partially sitting up, particularly if shortness of breath accompanies the heart attack.
3. Reassure him and stay with him.
4. When he is able to eat allow him a soft diet, preferably salt-free and about one quart of fluids per day.

Persons who are known to be subject to heart attacks usually carry with them the proper medication. If the attack is mild, they can give themselves the medication; if the attack is severe they may only be able to point to where the medication is. When administering medication be sure to read the label on the bottle first and give the victim only the prescribed amount.

Pain in the chest which is made more severe with deep breathing or coughing and has not been the immediate result of chest injury is often due to inflammation in the lung or chest cavity. A cloth binder pinned snugly about the chest, heat applied to the area of pain by a hot water bottle, and aspirin often provide some relief from the pain.

In the absence of chest injury, severe chest pain with pain in one or both arms or with symptoms of shock may mean heart trouble. If the sick person has had heart trouble previously, he will probably have a prescription and directions for its use from his private physician.

When severe chest pain is accompanied by symptoms of shock and there has been no obvious injury to the chest *do not* treat in the manner described for shock elsewhere in this handbook. You can, however, do the following things to help these persons and others having severe chest pain even though you do not know the exact cause of their illness:

Put the patient to bed. If he is having difficulty breathing, he should be propped up with pillows in a semi-sitting position. This position may make him more comfortable and his breathing easier. Give aspirin for pain.

The patient may be very fearful, with a sense of impending death. Reassurance is important to allay this fear. He should also be kept as quiet and as untouched by tension as is possible.

Light soft foods may be given in small helpings if desired, but do not force him to eat. Water or fruit juices may be given *in small quantities.*

A person who recovers from severe chest pain should continue to rest in bed until medical care is available.

HEAT ILLNESS

What To Do

1. Put the victim to bed or lay him down in a cool place.
2. Give him cool salted water to drink (1 teaspoonful of salt to 1 quart of water).

Caution: Do not give anything to an unconscious person.

Heat Exhaustion.—This condition may be mild or severe. In mild cases, the patient usually feels tired and may experience headache and nausea. In severe cases, perspiration is profuse, weakness extreme, and the skin is pale and clammy. *The temperature is usually normal or subnormal.* Vomiting may occur. Unconsciousness is rare, but often the patient will be unable to stand. Painful cramps in leg, or arm muscles may begin suddenly and continue for as long as 24 hours. *The patient's temperature is usually normal or subnormal.*

The excessive heat and high humidity which may exist in shelter living can affect your health. Preventive measures should be instituted in your shelter to avoid the onset of heat illness. Wear light, porous, loose-fitting clothing, and maintain adequate salt intake. Your salt intake can be increased by liberal use of salt on your food and can be further insured by salting your drinking water, using one level teaspoonful of salt to a gallon of water. This dilute solution is not unpleasant to taste.

Normally when the body is overheated, the excess heat is eliminated naturally through sweating and the cooling of the body surface by evaporation of sweat. In profuse sweating, however, large quantities of salt are lost and the essential salt balance of the body may be upset. Under conditions of high humidity and when tight or heavy clothing is worn, the cooling of the body surface by evaporation is sometimes interfered with. Under such circumstances, heat exhaustion, heat cramps, or heat stroke may occur.

Treatment for heat cramps should include giving the salt-water solution described in the treatment of heat exhaustion. Relief of cramps may also be obtained by massage of the cramping muscles, using firm pressure rather than vigorous kneading, and by applying warm, wet towels to the painful muscles.

HEAT STROKE

What To Do

1. Undress the person and put him to bed in the coolest available area.

2. Sponge body freely with water or alcohol to reduce his temperature to 102° F. or less.

3. To hold temperature at 102° F. or less damp sheets or blankets may be placed over the victim.

4. Administer salt solution as soon as it can be tolerated. (One half teaspoonful of salt in a glassful of water every 15 minutes for 3 hours.)

What Not To Do

DO NOT give stimulants such as coffee or tea.

Heat Stroke.—This is a serious condition. In contrast to heat exhaustion and heat cramps, a patient with heat stroke usually has a high fever (105 or higher), and no evident perspiration. His skin is hot and dry.

Symptoms include headache, dizziness, irritability, and seeing objects through a red or purplish haze. The patient may suddenly become unconscious, the pulse is full and strong, breathing is noisy like snoring, and there may be convulsions.

The first efforts in treatment of heat stroke should be to reduce the fever rapidly. Undress the patient and put him to bed in the coolest available area. Sponge his body freely with water or alcohol to reduce his temperature to 102° F. or less (by rectum). Vigorous efforts to reduce fever should be stopped when the body temperature reaches this point (102° F.), and the patient should then be observed for 10 minutes. The temperature may continue to decline or it may rise again. If it starts to rise, renew sponging cautiously.

Give no stimulants such as coffee or tea. Administer salt solution, as tolerated, and in the same way as described for heat exhaustion, provided the patient is fully conscious.

When the patient's temperature remains at relatively normal levels, cover him to the extent necessary and keep him in bed until fully recovered.

HERNIA

What To Do

1. Have person lie flat on his back with knees drawn up. This position makes the loop of bowel or other abdominal contents more likely to return to the abdomen and the swelling disappear.

2. If number 1 fails, have the person again lie on his back and apply cold compresses to the site of the hernia.

3. If numbers 1 and 2 fail to reduce the hernia, have the person turn over on his stomach and bring the knees up under the chest so that the buttocks are raised. Have him remain in this position for a few minutes to see if the hernia will be reduced.

What Not To Do

DO NOT attempt to push the hernia back into place with the fingers. This may cause serious damage.

DO NOT give any laxative or cathartic unless approved by a physician when communication is possible.

Hernias may appear in some persons following a disaster as they tend to overexert themselves causing severe muscular strain and from lifting, pushing, or jumping. These activities increase pressure within the abdomen and thus force out a section of bowel or other abdominal contents through an existing weak spot.

A painful swelling may appear suddenly. Swelling is tender to the touch and may range in size from that of a marble to a doubled up fist. In umbilical hernias the swelling appears at the navel (belly button). In femoral hernias just below the groin on the affected side. In inguinal hernias in the groin on the affected side. And hernias due to injury or surgical procedures, at the affected site.

A sharp stinging pain is felt at the moment of protrusion accompanied by a feeling of something "giving way" at the site of the hernia. Nausea or vomiting may occur at this time.

It is also possible that hernia may occur with little or no pain or discomfort. The person may first become aware of it by noting the appearance of a swelling of the site.

Follow the procedures shown under "What to Do" as above. If these methods of attempting to reduce the hernia fail, the person should be kept quiet as possible and should be cautioned about making any sudden movements or picking up anything other than extremely light objects. In the case of severe hernias, the person should be put to bed and cautioned to lie on his back as much as possible. Such complete relaxing may permit the hernia to reduce by itself. Aspirin may be given for pain. If the hernia is not reduced, the person should be placed on a soft diet and encouraged to drink ample amounts of fluids.

INSECT BITES

What To Do

BEES, WASPS, HORNETS

1. Remove the stinger.
2. Apply paste of baking soda (baking soda is available in medical kit).

SCORPIONS

1. Apply constricting band or tourniquet above the sting on the side toward the heart.
Caution: Remove after it has been in place about 5 minutes.
2. Apply ice pack if available; otherwise, cold wet cloths.
3. Keep person warm.
4. Keep affected arm or leg *lower* than rest of body for about 2 hours.

SPIDERS (BLACK WIDOW)

1. Keep person quiet.
2. Elevate hips and legs in shock position.
3. Apply hot packs if abdominal cramps develop.

Only a few spiders are considered poisonous to human beings. The black widow is apparently the only spider in the United States capable of causing death. The black widow is a glossy black covered with fine short hairs. The underside of the abdomen of the female has a characteristic red marking in the shape of an hourglass.

The female black widow spins her web in protective places such as dark corners of basement and between rocks. She stays near

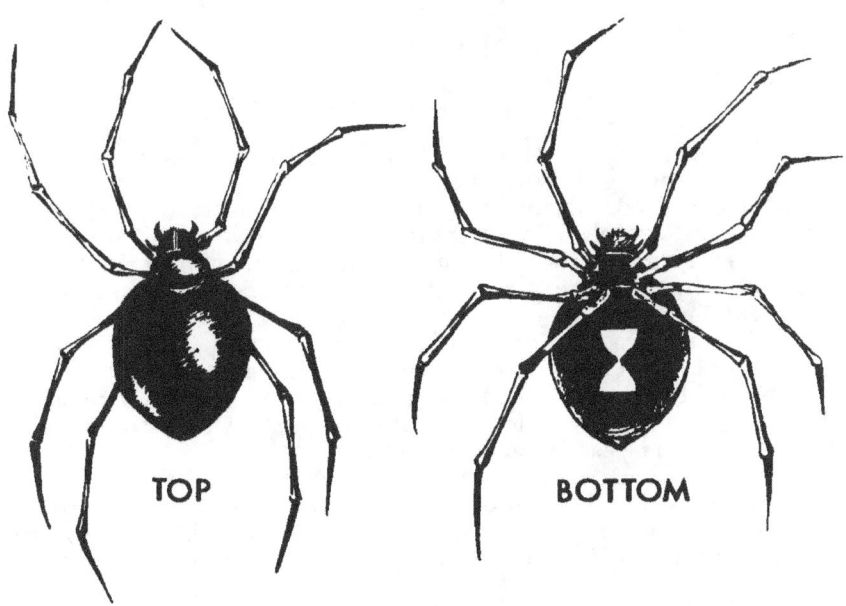

TOP   BOTTOM

her web ready to bite if disturbed. The much smaller male black widow is harmless.

At the time of the bite there is usually a sharp pain. The severity of the reaction depends upon the amount of venom that has been injected. The greater the amount the more severe the reaction.

Usually redness and local swelling develop immediately with serious poisoning pain developing almost at once in the region of the bite and spreading to the back and shoulders, chest, abdomen, and limbs.

The person should be kept quiet and warm, and lying down with hips and legs elevated in the shock position. If severe abdominal cramps develop heat may give some relief, such as hot water bottles or hot compresses.

It is estimated that only about 5 percent of black widow spider bites are fatal.

NAUSEA AND VOMITING

What To Do

1. Determine the cause if possible.
2. Put person to bed.
3. If cause can be determined refer to appropriate section of this manual.
4. Give warm liquid only when it can be tolerated.
5. If vomiting persists encourage person to take as much fluid as possible to prevent dehydration.
6. Start soft foods after liquids have been retained for 24 hours.

NOSEBLEED

What To Do

1. Place person in sitting position, head back *slightly*, and have him breathe through his mouth.
Note: Most nosebleeds will stop spontaneously. If bleeding continues try the following measures:
(*a*) Gently grasp the lower end of the nose between the thumb and index finger, firmly press the sides of the nose against the center for 5 minutes.
(*b*) Release pressure gradually.
(*c*) Apply cold cloths to back of neck or over nose.
Note.—If bleeding persists, plug the bleeding nostrils with small strip of gauze rolled up loosely. Leave part of roll sticking out of nose so it can be easily removed later.

Nosebleeds occur both spontaneously and as a result of injury. There may be an underlying disease, such as high blood pressure, but in many cases there is no disease. Some people, particularly young people, develop nosebleed following strenuous activity, colds, or exposure to high altitude. The bleeding is usually more annoying than serious. Occasionally, where disease is involved there may be sufficient bleeding to be dangerous.

Anyone with a nosebleed should remain quiet. A sitting position with head thrown back, or a lying position with head and shoulders raised, is best. Walking about, talking, laughing, or blowing the nose may cause increased bleeding or start bleeding again after it has stopped.

Usually the bleeding area is near the tip of the nose. Pinching the nostrils together puts pressure upon this area and helps to stop the flow. It may be necessary to pack the bleeding nostril lightly with gauze and then pinch. Sometimes it is necessary to maintain pressure with a small amount of gauze for several minutes, occasionally considerably longer.

PAIN

What To Do

1. Locate the pain area.
2. Determine its severity.
3. Determine, if possible, the cause.
4. If cause can be determined, refer to the appropriate section of this manual for care.
5. When cause cannot be determined, apply cold compresses to area of pain.
6. Give aspirin as directed on bottle.

Pain cannot be measured. Its severity can only be judged by what the individual experiencing the pain will say. Some people exaggerate the amount of pain they have; others can stand a great deal. Infants and young children cannot explain the type of pain they have; it is hard to determine where they have the pain and how severe it is. In all cases where pain is a symptom you should determine:
1. Where the pain is.
2. How long it has lasted.
3. Relation of pain to any specific activity.
4. Type of pain:
    (a) Dull.
    (b) Sharp.
    (c) Continuous.
    (d) Intermittent.
The above will assist you in determining the type of injury, or illness, that may be present and help you take the proper steps to try and relieve the pain.

In attempting to locate certain injuries, reference is made to pain or tenderness. There is a difference, which will be described here, as it may be of value to you at such time as it is necessary to describe a patient's condition through some means of communication to a physician, who may be located in another shelter. Pain usually falls into one of the categories. It is either dull, sharp, continuous, or intermittent. When lying still, the patient will have no control over the presence of the pain. When moving some part of his body, he may experience pain in specific locations; but when the movement is stopped, the pain will stop. *Tenderness*, however, is only experienced when the affected area is touched and some degree of pressure is applied. For example, in the case of some fractures, the patient—while lying still— may experience no pain; however, he will probably experience tenderness in the area of the fracture when the area is touched with the fingers and a slight pressure is applied.

Pain in the chest also can be serious. It may be accompanied by fever, coughing, or difficulty in breathing. It may indicate a congestion in the chest. A cloth binder pinned securely around the chest may make the person more comfortable. A hot water bag will also prove helpful.

Severe chest pain accompanied by signs of shock or pain in one, or both, arms may indicate heart trouble. Keep person lying down. If he is having difficulty in breathing, prop him up in a half-sitting position, or as high as he desires. Use pillows or whatever is available. He may breathe more easily and be more comfortable in this position.

If heart trouble is suspected, refer to appropriate section on "Heart Emergencies."

Pain in the Stomach

Although at times pain in the abdomen may be due only to a minor stomach upset, it should always be considered a sign of possible serious trouble.

A person with such pain should be kept warm and in bed. Cold, wet cloths should be applied to the abdomen. The patient should not be allowed to eat for at least two days if the pain keeps up. *No laxative should be given for it may make the trouble worse.*

POISONING
What To Do

WASH AND DILUTE

- MEDICINES
- INSECTICIDES
- DISINFECTANTS
- HOUSEHOLD CLEANERS
- RAT POISONS

NEUTRALIZE

- ACIDS
- ALKALIES

For general poisoning: Dilute with water; induce vomiting.

Universal antidote: 2 parts of activated charcoal, 1 part tannic acid, 1 part magnesium oxide. Mix 1 tablespoonful in ½ glass of water and give to patient. Such a mixture can be obtained from a drugstore and kept on hand for emergencies.

In acid (e.g., phenol, hydrochloric) and alkali (e.g., lye, ammonia, drainpipe cleaner) poisonings, dilute and neutralize, but DO NOT induce vomiting. Give milk, olive oil, or beaten egg whites. In petroleum distillates (e.g., kerosene, gasoline, lighter fluid) poisonings, DO NOT induce vomiting.

In a shelter where medical supplies, insecticides, and disinfectants are stored and conditions of life are abnormal, poisoning may occur. First aid must be given immediately; minutes count. The general aim is to dilute and remove the poison, to neutralize it by an antidote, and to help the body fight the poison. These measures are effective regardless of the kind of poison.

Quickly administer fluids in large amounts—four glassfuls or more for adults. Water usually is the most readily available. Milk is good as it will slow the absorption of many poisons. Either or both may be given. *Do not attempt to give fluids to an unconscious patient.*

In all cases—*except those involving special poisons*, described below, try to remove the poison from the patient's stomach immediately by inducing vomiting.

The larger the amount of fluid given, the greater the tendency to vomit. A strong salt solution—two tablespoonfuls to a glass of warm water—is nauseating and may be given repeatedly. Vomiting may also be induced in a conscious person by touching the back of the throat with the fingers or handle of a spoon. The patient should be placed face down with his head lower than his hips to prevent the matter vomited from entering his lungs and causing further damage.

If you can find the package from which the poison came, its antidote may be given on the label. If available without delay, use the antidote as directed.

If a specific antidote is not known, administer diluting fluids and carry out treatments as indicated above. After you have taken the most important steps, you may administer the universal antidote previously mentioned on page 67, or 1 or 2 tablespoonfuls of activated charcoal may be used in place of universal antidote. Mix with ½ glass of water and give to patient.

Unless the poison was a sedative (such as an overdose of sleeping tablets), have the patient lie down after he has vomited several times and keep him warm and quiet.

However, if the poison was a sedative, keep him awake by talking to him and encourage him to walk about. Give him several cups of black coffee every 2 hours until he gets better.

SPECIAL PROCEDURES FOR SPECIAL POISONS

Acids.—Dilute quickly with a glass of water and then give milk of magnesia, or if it is not available, baking soda solution, to neutralize the acid. Several glassfuls may be given *but do not give enough to cause vomiting.* Then give milk, olive oil, or egg white to protect the digestive tract lining.

Alkalies.—Give a glass of water quickly, then vinegar or lemon juice in the diluting fluid to neutralize the alkali. Follow with milk, olive oil, or egg white. *Do not cause vomiting.* The only reason for giving plain water first is that it is quickly available.

Kerosene Poisoning.—Give half cup of mineral oil, if available, to protect the digestive tract lining, and use strong coffee or tea as a stimulant. *Do not cause vomiting.* Keep the patient warm and combat shock. Be prepared to use artificial respiration if the patient stops breathing.

Carbon Monoxide Poisoning.—The problem is inhalation of gas, so the instructions for inducing or not inducing vomiting and other procedures given above do not apply.

It takes a combination of two causes to bring about carbon monoxide poisoning—the improper burning of fuel, and insufficient ventilation. In the emergency circumstances of shelter living, this combination may occur. Prevention is the best "treatment" but it may be difficult with improvised methods for heating and ventilation. If it is necessary to operate such things as furnace, fireplace, or space heater in your shelter, be sure that the ventilation is adequate.

Carbon monoxide gives no warning. You cannot see, taste, or smell the gas. It does not tickle the throat, make your eyes smart, or make its presence known in any obvious way. First symptoms—headache, nausea, dizziness, or a feeling of great sleepiness—have so many other causes you may tend to ignore them.

If poisoning does occur, get the victim to fresh air if possible. If he is not breathing or is breathing irregularly, start artificial respiration at once. Keep him warm and aid his circulation by rubbing his arms and legs. Avoid use of such stimulants as coffee or tea, and see that the patient has sufficient rest and time to recover in order to avoid strain on the heart.

RADIATION SICKNESS

The illness most closely associated with nuclear attack and fallout, and probably the one most dreaded by many people, is radiation sickness. You cannot see, taste, or feel the radiation that causes it, and so this illness seems mysterious and strange. However, although radiation adds a relatively new hazard to warfare, *it is not new and unfamiliar to medicine.*

X-ray burns and radiation sickness were recognized shortly after the discovery of X-rays themselves in 1895. The experience of watch dial painters in the Twenties showed the hazards of working with radioactive materials. In addition, there is abundant information from actual wartime experience in Japan and from the use of radioactive materials in medical care in many clinics in this country.

Nuclear radiation damages body cells by causing chemical changes in them. The amount of damage depends on the amount of radiation received and the period of time during which the body is exposed.

Since the body repairs some of the radiation damage, an individual can receive a given amount of radiation over a period of weeks without being incapacitated, whereas the same amount received in a few days would cause serious illness. As a matter of fact we get some radiation every day from the air, and periodically from such things as medical and dental uses of X-ray, without apparent harm. It is concentrated and continued exposure that is dangerous. Most persons suffering from mild or moderate exposure will recover.

If you take advantage of the fallout shelter program and heed the warnings that will be available to you concerning the direction and approach of radioactive fallout following an attack, you should be able to avoid the kind of exposure that is dangerous.

If you *must* leave your shelter, protect yourself with additional outer clothing while outside. On returning, remove the extra outer clothing before entering the shelter and cleanse yourself carefully. This will help prevent your bringing radioactive fallout particles into the shelter.

The usual symptoms of radiation sickness are lack of appetite, nausea, vomiting, fatigue, drowsiness, weakness (sometimes extreme), headache, sore mouth, loss of hair, bleeding gums, diarrhea, and bleeding under the skin.

Persons with these symptoms should be treated as if they have been exposed to radiation. But in order to avoid undue anxiety, you should realize that *not everyone who has nausea or vomiting, fatigue, or weakness has radiation sickness.* These conditions may come from just plain anxiety and the tension likely to arise in a crowded shelter at the time of a disaster.

It is important also for you to know that *radiation sickness is not contagious.* You will be in no danger of "catching it" by caring for a person suffering from it in your shelter, provided the fallout particles have been removed from his clothing, body, and hair.

The severity of radiation sickness varies according to the amount of exposure and a person's individual reaction to radiation. However, in general, radiation sickness can be mild, moderate, or severe, as described below.

Mild Exposure.—Most people who receive enough exposure to produce mild radiation sickness will show no immediate symptoms. However, a few particularly sensitive persons in this group of the mildly exposed may show some early signs of illness—upset stomach, lack of appetite, and fatigue—within a few hours of exposure. They should be encouraged to rest but can continue regular activities. Recovery should be prompt and complete.

Moderate Exposure.—Symptoms of radiation sickness from moderate exposure will appear in about two hours. A patient may have an upset stomach, rather sudden in its beginning, with nausea, lack of appetite, fatigue, and drowsiness.

During the first day, distress will probably increase. Vomiting, extreme weakness, and even prostration may occur. The symptoms will usually disappear toward the end of the day, but the nausea and vomiting may recur on the second day. By the third day, the person will often feel normal.

No further symptoms may appear, and the person may feel able to work and carry out all the duties of an unexposed person. But rest and reduced activity should be encouraged for a few days. In persons more sensitive to radiation, vomiting and weakness may continue for a longer period.

Severe Exposure.—Persons who have been more seriously exposed develop all of the early symptoms described. After 2 or 3 days, their vigor and appetite will probably return, but during the second week, fever soreness in the mouth and diarrhea may appear. The gums and mouth may show signs of ulcers or bleeding. There may also be loss of hair in some persons although this does not usually take place until the third week.

In cases of overwhelming exposure, death may occur in hours or days. Those who recover from severe exposure may suffer from fever and mouth ulcers for periods as long as 7 or 8 weeks.

Treatment of Radiation Sickness

Emergency treatment deals with the symptoms of the illness.
Headache.—Give an adult 1 to 2 aspirin tablets every 3 or 4 hours. For children, ½ aspirin every 3 or 4 hours.
Nausea.—Motion sickness tablets may be given in dosage previously prescribed by your doctor.
Vomiting and Diarrhea.—Encourage the patient to take liquid as soon as possible to make up for the fluid he loses through vomiting and diarrhea. Fluids should be started even though attacks of vomiting continue to occur. A salt and soda solution is valuable for this fluid replacement. It is prepared by adding 1 teaspoonful of table salt and ½ teaspoonful baking soda to 1 quart of cool water. *The patient should drink this solution slowly.* When vomiting has ceased the patient should be taking at least 6 to 8

cups of liquid a day. The salt and soda solution can be alternated with bouillon and fruit juices. Children will require less liquid.
Weakness.—Weakness is frequently associated with vomiting and diarrhea. Put the patient to bed and keep him warm and quiet.
Sore Mouth.—Use a mild salt solution mouth wash (½ teaspoonful to a quart of water). Give aspirin for pain and discomfort.

SKIN RASH

What To Do

1. To relieve itching apply compress soaked in cool soda solution (3 teaspoons of baking soda and a glass of cool water).
2. For rashes with small pimples or eruptions cover generously with paste of bicarbonate of soda.
3. Caution person not to scratch or rub area.

Skin rashes may be a sign of serious illness.
If skin rash is combined with cold symptoms in a child, it may mean one of the communicable diseases of childhood.
The child should be isolated as much as possible and put to bed. He should be given as much fluid as possible to drink and be kept warm. If he has a fever, see treatment under "Fever."
Itching of the skin may be reduced by applying a baking soda solution. Put three teaspoonfuls of baking soda in a glass of water. (If you have soda tablets, use as directed on package.) Soak a cloth in the solution and lay the cloth on the itchy area. The cooler the solution, the greater the relief.

STROKE (APOPLEXY)

What To Do

1. Put the person to bed, propped up on pillows if he is more comfortable.
2. When breathing is difficult, turn his face to one side so fluid may drain from his mouth.
3. Remove any loose dental bridges or false teeth.

Note: See also—Heat Stroke and/or Heat Illness.

Stroke is caused by a rupture or blockage of a tiny blood vessel in the brain. It occurs more frequently in elderly people. The person may faint, the face becomes very flushed and he often breathes noisily. The pupils of the eyes may be unequal in size, his speech may be affected so that it is blurred or stumbling. One side of his body, or parts of one side, may become paralyzed.
Keep the person in bed. He does not need to lie flat but may be more comfortable propped up on a pillow. If he is unconscious, keep him flat. If he has difficulty in breathing turn him on his side and allow secretion to drain from his mouth. Any loose

dental bridges or false teeth should be removed. If the stroke is not too severe he will recover. If it is severe the person may become unconscious and die without regaining consciousness. Most people recover from a slight stroke. They should be kept in bed, given fluids and soft foods which they can take easily and be kept as comfortable as possible. Allow them to move around, sit up or get up if they desire when their strength returns. Partial paralysis may be present and persist after other symptoms have subsided. Move and turn the person as much as possible to prevent bed sores or congestion in the chest. Prop the person up or let him sit up in a chair if it is possible for him to move.

TOOTHACHE

What To Do

1. If available, apply oil of cloves or toothache drops (from medical kit) on a small piece of cotton and gently pack into the tooth cavity. Repeat two or three times daily.
2. Ice packs or hot packs may provide relief.
3. One-half ounce of whiskey, or similar alcoholic beverage, held in the mouth next to the sore tooth for about 5 minutes.
4. Aspirin may be used to relieve the pain.
5. Apply hot packs to the cheek on the side of the aching tooth.

UNCONSCIOUSNESS

What To Do

(When Person Is Flushed—Red Faced—With Strong Slow Pulse)

Lay person down with head *slightly raised* above level of rest of body.
Apply cold wet cloth to head.
If breathing stops start artificial respiration.

(When Person Is Pale—Cold—Clammy to Touch—With Weak Pulse)

Lay person down with head *slightly lower* than rest of body.
Keep him warm.
If available hold aromatic spirit of ammonia under nose (except where head injury is suspected).
If breathing stops start artificial respiration.

(When Person Has Bluish-Face, Weak Pulse, Irregular Breathing)

Lay person down.
Keep him warm.
Start artificial respiration immediately if breathing stops.

What Not To Do

DO NOT give stimulant.
DO NOT give food or drink.
DO NOT move (except to remove from danger).

Unconsciousness may occur in such conditions as fainting, apoplexy (sometimes called a stroke), shock, and diabetes. (See treatment of shock, and discussion of diabetes.)

Simple fainting occurs when not enough blood reaches the brain. This may be due to hunger, fatigue, emotional distress, or severe injury.

Warnings of faintness are blurring of the vision, weakness, paleness, and giddiness. If you should have these symptoms, lie down immediately if possible. If not, sit or kneel and bend forward at the waist, putting your head down to get it lower than your heart.

A person who has fainted should be kept flat with no pillow under his head. His feet should be elevated. Be sure he is breathing without difficulty. (If not, use the same measures as described below for the stroke patient.) Usually he will recover in a few minutes without any further care. He should rest for some time after recovery.

Apoplexy (or stroke) should be suspected whenever an elderly person faints. Apoplexy is caused by interference with the blood supply to the brain. It may occur when a blood vessel in the brain bursts or becomes blocked.

Sometimes a person with apoplexy will collapse but not completely lose consciousness. His face may become red and congested. One side of his body or parts of one side may become paralyzed. His speech may be affected, blurred, and stumbly. He may have difficulty swallowing.

Where stroke is suspected, the sick person should be kept in bed but he does not need to lie flat. He can be propped comfortably with pillows. However, if he is unconscious, he should be placed flat in bed on his back or either side. To avoid bed sores, his position in bed should be changed every four hours. Remove any loose dental bridges or false teeth from his mouth. If secretions collect in the back of his mouth and interfere with breathing, he should be placed on his side and the secretion allowed to drain from his mouth.

Most persons recover from a slight stroke. If the stroke is severe, unconsciousness sometimes continues for days and days and death may result.

INFANT AND CHILD CARE

CARE OF THE NEW BABY

Nothing should be done to the baby's eyes, ears, nose, or mouth. The baby should not be washed or cleaned in any way the first day. He will be covered with a thin, white, waxy material. This material will be unpleasant looking and will soon have an unpleasant odor but it will act as a protective covering for the baby's skin and protect it against infection better than any cleaning. It also helps the baby adjust to the change in temperature between the mother's womb and the outside world.

If there is enough water, each person who handles the baby should wash his hands first.

Try to keep everyone away from the baby except those who are taking care of him. This is especially true of other children. If it is possible, do not let anyone who has a cold or seems to be sick take care of the baby.

The newborn baby will cry occasionally but will sleep most of the time. His color will tend to be pink but may be somewhat bluish the first day or two, especially the hands and feet. His skin may have a mottled appearance.

The baby may appear jumpy and have jerky motions, especially if startled by noise or handling. His breathing may be very quiet or, at times, rattling or snoring as if he has mucus in his throat or nose. This is quite normal and should not worry the mother.

The baby should be kept comfortably warm and wrapped in a clean towel or sheet. If the shelter area is very hot, avoid excessive covering.

The newborn baby needs very little care during the first few days of life. He can get along without food or water for two days or longer.

During the first week or two, slight yellowish material may come from his eyes. The first bowel movements will be black or greenish in color and then become light yellow and rather soft.

Girl babies may have a thick white, yellowish, or bloody discharge from the vagina. Babies sometimes develop swelling and discharge of milk fluid from the breasts. These things are normal and nothing needs to be done about them.

FEEDING THE BABY

Breast feeding would be the most practical method of feeding a baby in a shelter. But it should not be tried if the mother's health is not up to it or if she does not expect to receive an adequate amount of food and fluids.

The nipple and the part of the mother's breast around the nipple should be bathed once a day with mild soap and water, rinsed, and dried gently with cotton or a soft cloth.

Some mothers prefer demand feeding, which means feeding the baby whenever his cries indicate hunger. Other mothers prefer a more or less fixed schedule. Either arrangement is all right for the baby. A suggested schedule for those who prefer one would be to put the baby to the breast at birth, again 12 hours and 24 hours later, then every 8 hours during the second day, every 4 hours during the third and fourth days, and every 3 or 4 hours after that.

During the first few days, the baby should be put to the mother's breast for no more than 3 or 4 minutes at each feeding on one breast. After that, feeding need not last more than about 10 minutes in order to get the milk the baby needs. The baby, however, may prefer to remain longer for comfort and cuddling.

The mother should alternate breasts, one per feeding. If the baby does not seem to get enough milk, she may try giving the baby both breasts at each feeding. If that still does not seem to supply enough milk after several days, as shown by the baby's cries after feedings, artificial feeding should be started.

MAKING A FORMULA

For artificial feeding, the simplest method is to use evaporated milk (unsweetened canned) diluted with water. During the first two weeks after birth, the formula should be two parts water to one part evaporated milk.

If no water is available and the family is living on fluids from food and fruit, the baby can take the evaporated milk with no water added. But he will need smaller amounts and will need fruit juice or other bland liquids at other times during the day.

The bottle and nipple should be cleaned as well as possible, preferably boiled. The milk should be poured directly in the bottle and the water added in the bottle.

Any unused milk should be kept in a refrigerator or cool place. If there is no cool storage place, the left-over milk should be used right away by some other person.

If no feeding bottle, nipple, and means of measuring are available, estimate the two parts of water to one part of evaporated milk in a glass. Then pour the mixture into a bowl and feed the baby with a teaspoon. Place the tip of the spoon against the baby's lower lip so that the baby can suck on the spoon. If it is poured in, the baby will gasp and choke on it.

If a medicine dropper is available, use this to drop milk slowly into the inside of the baby's cheek.

Keep the bottle, bowl, and other materials scrupulously clean between feedings and use for nothing else. The baby's formula does not necessarily have to be heated.

During the first two weeks, most of the baby's crying will be due to hunger. If the baby cries immediately after feeding, it usually means he wants more. Offer him more. He will not take more than he wants.

If a baby cries between feedings, he may be thirsty, especially if the shelter is hot. Give the baby water several times a day between feedings.

A baby does not need vitamins during the first few weeks.

BODY CARE FOR BABY

Waterproof panties or substitutes, such as oilcloth or plastic material, should be used in order to avoid wetting the surface on which the baby lies. If diapers, torn up sheets, or other diaper substitutes are not available, you can make a filler out of paper towels, napkins, or toilet tissue.

After 24 hours the baby can be bathed. Baby oil may be used, if water is scarce. Soiled parts should be wiped gently and thoroughly with a damp cloth or cotton dipped in baby oil. Unless the skin is very irritated, diapers do not have to be changed after each wetting but should be changed after bowel movements.

If a sterile dressing has been available for covering the stump of the cord at the navel, this covering should be continued until the cord dries up and falls off. This usually occurs in a week. No other treatment is necessary.

PREMATURE BABY

If the baby is born before it is due and is very small, he will sleep most of the time. He may look bluer than other babies. *The most important thing is to keep him warm.* If the shelter is cold, it may be wise to wrap the baby and place him inside the mother's clothing or bed for her body heat. If this is done, precautionary measures should be taken to prevent suffocation.

It may be possible to keep him warm with hot water bottles in a large box into which a smaller box may be placed for his bed. Be careful not to burn the baby.

The premature baby needs very little food—nothing at all for 2 or 3 days. If he seems strong enough to suck at the mother's breast, that should be tried. Otherwise, use a spoon or a medicine dropper in the manner described in the section "Making a Formula."

The very small baby may need to be fed every 2 or 3 hours. He may be able to take only one or two teaspoons of the evaporated milk and water mixture at a time. If he spits up, he is probably getting too much.

Bed may be made from drawer, box, basket, etc. It should be heated with warm bricks, bottles, stones, or similar items. Be very careful not to use next to baby and run risk of burning him. A small box may be put inside a larger box with heated articles between. Pad and line with newspapers and cloth or blankets, and cover the structure with a blanket to keep heat in.

MEDICAL AND FIRST-AID SUPPLIES

Medical supplies must be tailored to the individual needs of your family. Existing health problems in the family, such as diabetes, heart disease, asthma, or peptic ulcer, may make it necessary to include certain specific medicines in your supply.

If there are infants or children in your family, you may need such things as baby oil and baby powder. If anyone in the family is pregnant, you must be prepared with supplies for emergency delivery and after-care of mother and child. (See "Expectant Mother's Emergency Childbirth Kit.") Elderly members of the family may have special needs.

In addition to special items dictated by family health problems and, to a certain extent, by the age of family members, there is a basic list of medical and first aid supplies recommended for all. You are urged to discuss this basic list, as well as your special needs, with your doctor so that he may suggest specific medicines to buy, provide you with prescriptions, if necessary, and advise you regarding quantities you will need, how to use the medicines, how to store them, and how long they can be stored without important deterioration.

List of Basic Supplies

Antiseptic solution
Aspirin tablets (5 grain)
Baking soda
Cough mixture
Diarrhea medication
Ear drops
Table salt
Toothache remedy
First aid handbook
Pregnancy supply
Specific medications recommended by your physician
Adhesive tape, roll (2" wide)
Applicators, sterile, cotton-tipped
Bandage, sterile roll (2" wide)
Bandage, sterile roll (4" wide)
Bandages, triangular (37"x37"x52")
Bandages (can of plastic strips, assorted sizes)
Cotton, sterile, absorbent

Laxative
Motion sickness tablets
Nose drops (water soluble)
Petroleum jelly
Rubbing alcohol
Smelling salts
Dressings, sterile (4"x4")
Hot water and enema bag (combination with syringe attachment)
Medicine dropper
Safety pins (assorted sizes)
Sanitary napkins
Soap
Scissors
Splints, wooden (18" long)
Thermometer (clinical oral or rectal type)
Tweezers
Water purification materials

CARE AND MAINTENANCE OF SUPPLIES

Medicines obtained for your emergency supply should be so labeled that the name of the medicine, instructions for use, and necessary warnings, such as "for external use only" and "POISON," are clearly visible. These medicines should be carefully packed to prevent breakage. *They should be stored out of reach of children* in a dry, cool space. Best storage temperature should be below 70 degrees, but they should not be frozen.

Some medicines may have to be replaced periodically. If a medicine which deteriorates on storage is one frequently used by your family in normal circumstances, you can replace your emergency supply of it from time to time with currently purchased supplies, and use the older medicine from your disaster kit before its expiration date.

Where shelters have been provisioned by the Federal government, Medical Kits containing the following items are included:

Medication

Aspirin
Sodium Chloride
Sodium Bicarbonate
Cascara, Sagrada ext. tablets
Phenobarbital sodium tablets
Soap, surgical
Sulfadiazine tablets
Eugenol
Tablet Water Purification
Kaolin and Pectin Mixture
Penicillin G tablets
Isopropyl Alcohol
Eye, nose drops
Vaseline

Dressings

Bandage, Gauze Rolls
Bandage, muslin
Cotton, purified
Pad, gauze, surgical

Other

Applicator, wood, cotton-tipped end
Depressor, tongue, wood
Forceps, splinter, tweezer
Thermometer, human, clinical, oral
Thermometer, human, clinical, rectal
Pin, safety, medium
Syringe, fountain, plastic and attachments
Scissors, pocket
Belts, sanitary

OTHER EMERGENCY SUPPLIES

Can and bottle openers
Knives, forks, spoons
Pans for cooking and washing
Paper plates and paper towels
Small, compact cooking unit, such as those used by campers
Candles
Flashlights, electric lantern, and spare batteries
Matches—safety and/or kitchen matches in waterproof case
Clock
Radio—portable battery type, with extra batteries
Blankets
Pillows and pillow cases
Extra clothing, such as coveralls for use if you must go outside your shelter—include rubbers to cover your shoes and hat or scarf for your head

Sheets
Personal toiletries
Broom
Dust pan
Fly swatter
Rags for cleaning
String and rope
Hammer and nails
Pliers
Screwdriver and screws
Shovel—for digging way out, if necessary, and for burying wastes
Wrench—open-end adjustable
Pail of sand for fire fighting and sanitation
Fire extinguisher
Games
Paper, pen, pencils, crayons
Reading materials
Sewing kit

NOTES

Emergency Medical Identification

Learn to recognize this symbol. It may save a life or lessen disability. Worn as a bracelet, necklace or anklet, it means that the bearer has special health needs if he is injured or suddenly taken ill. A card in pocket or purse will explain the patient's special needs. Everyone with special medical problems, or who takes medicines regularly, or who has dangerous allergies, or who requires any special medical attention at all—such as the hard of hearing, contact lens wearers, non-English speakers—should wear the Emergency Medical Identification symbol and carry an Emergency Medical Identification card.